MINI
MASTERPIECES

LAURA LOHMANN

THIS BOOK IS DEDICATED TO MY FAMILY.
I HAVE BEEN BLESSED THROUGH THE YEARS
TO HAVE A FAMILY THAT ALWAYS ENCOURAGES
ME TO FOLLOW MY DREAMS AND PASSIONS.
MAY YOU FIND THIS BOOK AN INSPIRATION
AND REMEMBER TO KEEP ON CREATING!

Text and images copyright © 2020 by Laura Lohmann.
Cover image by Holly Aprecio of Holly Aprecio Photography.

Published by
The Innovation Press
1001 Fourth Avenue, Suite 3200
Seattle, WA 98154
www.theinnovationpress.com

Printed by Worzalla.
Production Date: July 2020

10 9 8 7 6 5 4 3 2 1

ISBN: 9781943147830
Library of Congress Control Number: 2020936005

Typesetting by Kerry Ellis.

CONTENTS

INTRODUCTION

Artists through the ages have drawn their inspiration from many sources when creating their personal masterpieces. Some of their sources of inspiration can be found in nature and flowers, city or country landscapes, or shapes and bold bright colors. Many have also drawn inspiration from the artists who came before them. I have always been inspired by great artists and their works. Sometimes inspiration comes from the subject matter of a painting, or an artist's use of vivid color, or a specific material they used to create their masterpiece.

Through my experience creating art with children, I have found that some children may be excited about the subject matter or the use of a new art material, but quite often they are drawn to art simply for the process of creating.

Art is a language that lets us develop our thoughts, express our ideas and emotions, and nurture our soul. For children, it helps develop their mind and creative process. When children create art, it stimulates both sides of the brain and it gives them the chance to explore and express themselves. I hope you enjoy the process of creating and find inspiration in this book while you create your mini-masterpieces.

Laura xox

HOW TO USE THIS BOOK

This book contains fifty-two projects inspired by specific artists and their artwork, both past and present. The projects are divided into four categories. These categories represent themes that come up often in artists' artwork. Projects are geared for various ages with the time allotted for each. Each project also contains a brief biography about the artist and a list of supplies needed.

A simple list of art materials for these projects includes:

- Drawing paper
- Construction paper
- Watercolor paper
- Tissue paper
- Tempera paint
- Watercolor paint
- Paintbrushes
- Glue
- Scissors
- Chalk
- Oil pastels
- Clay

These supplies are readily available at craft and large retail stores. A comprehensive list of recommended art supplies is available in the appendix at the back of the book. Step-by-step instructions with full-color photos are included for each project, but you can easily adapt any of them to meet your needs and interests. For example, a project using paint could also be done in oil pastels. Get a feel for a project before presenting it to the children. This will help you become more comfortable with the materials, give you confidence as an instructor, and make you aware of where any frustrations might arise. I also encourage you to adapt the ideas and materials suggested in this book. As you become more comfortable with the materials, you might find yourself less reliant on presenting themes and allowing younger children to explore with the art materials. Projects do not need to be done in any particular order. Just as an artist changes colors, subject matter, or ideas, children will want to select different projects. Feel free to jump around and create those that they find most interesting.

Before beginning a project, I suggest exploring just a little bit about a particular artist and their life experiences. This can give insight into the inspirations for some of the most famous and unique works of art in the world. Many artists' lives are rich with detail. Creating art with the knowledge of an artist or a painting helps a child make a connection to that artist's world, other cultures, and helps the child express their feelings and life experiences.

Many of the projects in this book list publications for further reading as well as some of the artists' other notable works. This will help children connect with established artists. Knowing the story behind a painting or an artist may change a viewpoint or spur a new idea.

The projects in this book are geared for children ages five through twelve, but people of any age can create a beautiful masterpiece using these steps, with some guidance if needed. Be assured that both boys and girls will find interest in these projects and techniques, while learning some basic background information about a variety of artists.

10 TIPS FOR PREPARING YOUR CREATIVE SPACE

Art can be made anywhere, anytime, but making a special space for children to create will keep your art materials organized and help promote an inspirational journey. Here are my simple tips for setting up a creative space:

1. Designate a small table to use for creating your projects. This will come in handy when art-work needs to dry overnight.
2. Start a collection of books that showcase various artists. Store these books near your art space. You can find awesome books at museum gift shops, bookstores, libraries, and even resale shops.

3. Use a cart with shelves to store your paints and brushes. Small, multi-shelved utility carts on casters work great.
4. I have my paint cabinets neatly organized by colors for quick access. I also prefer to premix colors ahead of time. A secret I use when mixing is to add a little drop of yellow to warm colors and greens. This will make the colors brighter. Don't forget that colors can be made lighter by mixing in some white paint. This creates a tint of the original color. Just like a good recipe might call for heavy cream, make sure you use premium tempera paint and not watered down or washable tempera, especially when working with children over six years old. For children under six years old, washable tempera paint is fine. Children of this age are more excited about the process than the end result.

5. I have a huge assortment of paintbrushes separated into containers. Always store brushes with the bristles up.
6. Cover worktables with craft paper. This will help protect tabletops and aid in cleanup.
7. Organize supplies in clear plastic bins with labels to help children find needed supplies quickly and easily.

8. Use heavyweight manila tagboard as placemats underneath painting projects. If you can't locate big sheets of tagboard, try using scrap cardboard instead. It works great as well.
9. Prepare art materials in advance. Have paints mixed, paper cut, and tools organized so children can create at any time. For projects that require a water rinse between paints, I like to use weighted dog bowls as water containers to prevent spills.

10. If you're working with a larger group, you'll notice that some children work at a faster pace than others. I always have various sculptural supplies such as blocks available for children who finish early.

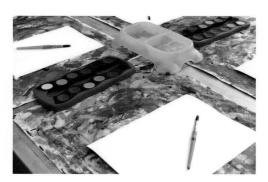

TEMPERA PAINTING WITH CHILDREN IS AS EASY AS 1, 2, 3

I have been teaching art to children for more than twenty years. Keeping paint colors vibrant has become my specialty and one of the things I am most often asked about. People shy away from using tempera paint due to the mess. Over the years I've developed an easy painting technique for children that involves three simple steps to eliminate this problem.

1. Place a painting placemat (tagboard, poster board, or thin cardboard) on a clean, uncluttered table with a piece of art paper on top of the placemat. This placemat will designate the spot for your child to create. Each child should have their own placemat.

2. Dispense tempera paint in plastic or Styrofoam egg cartons or ice cube trays. If using Styrofoam egg cartons, cover small holes at the bottom with masking tape to avoid leakage. Always have a piece of tagboard or a tray under your paint trays. When dispensing the paint, start on one side of the container and always begin with the lightest colors. Yellows and tans should be filled first. Oranges, reds, and greens are next. Blues and purples are better toward the opposite end of the paint carton.

TIP: Dispensing the paint in this order will help children from becoming confused about which color to use next, and it will keep the colors from becoming muddy.

When painting with children, unless the project calls for brown or black paint, it is best to exclude those colors from the paint tray. Black should always be last, unless used first, and left to dry before using other colors. Teach children to use this color order when painting. Once lighter colors have been used, continue working down the paint tray toward the darkest colors.

3. Teach children to keep the tempera paint on the tip of the brush. This will keep the paint from saturating the bristles and provides more control of the paint on the paper. Not using water to clean brushes in between colors will eliminate spills and keep the paint from becoming watered down and dull. Instead of using water to clean brushes, wipe any excess paint onto the outer edge of the tagboard painting placemat.

TIP: When done, cover the tray with tin foil to keep the paint from drying out.

HOW TO MAKE PAINTED PAPER

Some activities in this book will call for painted paper. Making painted paper is an art form all its own. Children love the creative freedom when applying paint to various papers, especially construction paper. This process-based art creates various implied textures on paper. Scraping, tapping, smearing, and splattering are just a few techniques to use when creating painted paper. Make sure to make plenty of painted paper ahead of time to be stored for future use.

WHAT YOU WILL NEED

- Tagboard, poster board, or thin cardboard

- Shallow plate or bowl

- Tempera paint in white and two analogous colors

- 12" x 18" colored construction paper

- Large round paintbrush

- Other paint applicators such as scrapers, cardboard, texture brushes, or padded stampers can be used instead of paintbrushes

Set up the space with a placemat and tempera paint in a bowl or on a shallow plate. Use white and two analogous colors. Analogous colors are colors next to each other on the color wheel.

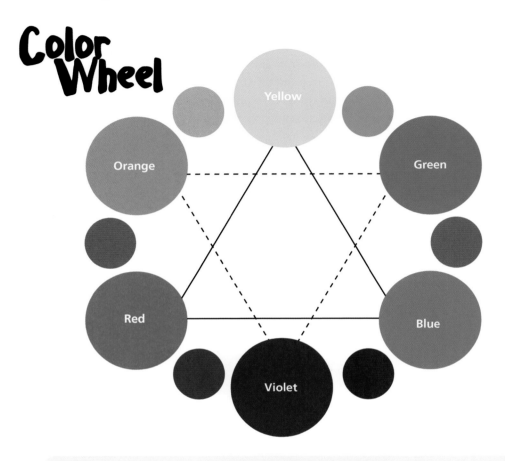

 The **primary colors** are red, yellow and blue.

 The **secondary colors** are orange, violet and green.

- **Complementary colors** are opposites on the color wheel. Placing complementary colors next to each other enhances them.

- **Analogous colors** are colors that sit side by side on the color wheel and have a common hue. For example, orange, yellow and green are analogous because they all have yellow in common.

- **Warm colors** are red, yellow and orange. **Cool colors** are blue, green and violet.

- **Intensity** refers to the brightness of a color. To lower the intensity of a color, mix it with its complement.

- A **tint** is any color plus white.

- A **shade** is any color plus black.

Dip a large round brush into the paint. On a piece of 12" x 18" colored construction paper, hop the brush around, creating overlapping paint splotches that extend to the edge of the paper. Using colored construction paper adds additional color underneath the paint. I prefer to dip into one color paint at a time but there is no right or wrong method. Double dipping is OK, just be sure not to stir the paint colors on the plate or in the bowl. When creating painted paper, it is not necessary to clean your brush in between colors.

Use of other paint applicators will give different textures and designs. Encourage children to create patterns or an all-over design. A spray bottle with watered-down paint works great for small spots. Exploring with various tools and paints is always a favorite activity for children.

I reuse the tagboard placemats until they are completely covered in paint. After that they become painted paper to be used on future projects.

DISPLAYING YOUR MASTERPIECES

Children just beam with delight when their artwork is displayed. Not only does it fill them with pride, it shows that you value their art and that you care about them.

Displaying art also makes your space beautiful. Art should be shared. It's important to talk about the art your children create, and to ask questions about the process and what materials they used.

Some tools for displaying artwork include:

- Cork board with tacks or push pins
- Washi tape
- Magnets on magnetic boards
- Command clips

STAINED GLASS WINDOW

INSPIRED BY: *Magnolia and Irises* (1908) by Louis Comfort Tiffany
AGE: 9–12 years
PROJECT DURATION: 120 minutes plus overnight drying

ABOUT THE ARTIST

Louis Comfort Tiffany (February 18, 1848–January 17, 1933) was an American painter, craftsman, decorator, and designer. He is known internationally for his contributions to the art of glassmaking and his association with Art Nouveau, an ornamental style of art popular between 1890 and 1910. His experimentation with stained glass in 1875 led to the creation of the Tiffany Glass and Decorating Company. His business served wealthy residents of New York, the Cathedral of St. John the Divine in New York City, and even the White House. Around 1896 Tiffany became interested in blown glass. He began using this glass in the production of his famous jewelry, lamps, and pottery, which are of high value today.

WET ON WET WATERCOLOR TECHNIQUE

To achieve a blurred or tie-dyed look on your background paper, apply water on the watercolor paper, then apply watercolor paints on top of the wet paper. This will move the watercolor in different directions.

SUPPLIES

- Watercolor paper (9" x 12")
- Paintbrush (medium round)
- Watercolors (turquoise, blue)
- Container of water
- Painted paper or construction paper (shades of light gray, brown, blue, purple, green)
- Glue (sponges)
- Scissors
- Permanent marker (black)
- Painting placemat

1. Background Paper

   Position a piece of watercolor paper vertically and brush small amounts of water on top. Be careful not to oversaturate the paper. Apply turquoise and blue watercolors onto the wet paper with a paintbrush. Apply more blue paint at the top and bottom of the paper. Let dry overnight.

2. Background Hills, Iris Stems, and Trees

   A. Cut sloping hill shapes out of dark blue shades of painted paper and glue them down in the middle part of the background paper. Repeat this process and make shorter hills out of a lighter piece of painted paper. Glue the lighter paper hills in front of the darker paper hills. (Refer to How to Make Painted Paper on page 9. Refer to How to Make Glue Sponges on page 225).

   B. Add overlapping, thin strips of green paper to create the stems of the irises.

   C. Create two tree trunks out of thin strips of gray or brown painted paper and place one on each side of the background paper in a vertical position. Make sure the trunks touch the bottom of the background paper. Use the same color of painted paper to add smaller branches extending from the tree trunks.

3. Flowers and Stained Glass Effect

   A. Use purple painted paper or construction paper to add flowers to the top of the iris stems. Use a yellow oil pastel for the center of the flower. With a shade of light gray painted paper or construction paper, add small flowers or blossoms on the trees. A small heart shape works nicely. Overlap the flowers to create a fully blooming tree.

   B. Use a black permanent marker and outline all the shapes. This will create the famous Tiffany stained glass look.

OPTION FOR YOUNGER ARTISTS

Use a piece of 12" x 18" construction paper for the background. Glue strips of various shades of green construction paper at the bottom to create the iris stems. Cut simple shapes out of purple paper to create the flowers and glue on top of the stems. Outline with black permanent marker.

ADDITIONAL ARTWORK

The Four Seasons (1900)

Bowl (1898-1902)

Pond Lily Library Lamp (1905)

CLAY SUNFLOWERS

INSPIRED BY: *Sunflowers* (1889) by Vincent Van Gogh
AGE: 6 years and up
PROJECT DURATION: 120 minutes plus 3 or more days of drying time

ABOUT THE ARTIST

Vincent Van Gogh (March 30, 1853–July 29, 1890) was a Dutch painter and one of the most well-known artists in the world. Many people of his time found his behavior eccentric, isolating Van Gogh and creating a difficult life for him. Since people didn't understand him, he unsuccessfully held many jobs until age twenty-seven when he decided to become a painter. Painting landscapes was his main interest, though when the weather was bad and he couldn't paint outside, he worked in his studio creating still-life paintings. Sunflowers were Van Gogh's favorite subject to paint. In the late summer of 1887 he made his first study of these golden flowers in the fields around Paris. He experimented with bright shades of yellow and orange, and how the colors changed when placed next to each other. Van Gogh liked working with bold colors and applied his paint in thick layers, often directly from the tube. The thick paint and visible brushstrokes give the surface of his paintings a bumpy appearance.

SUPPLIES

- Air dry clay
- Wooden craft stick or Popsicle stick to cut the clay
- Cup of water
- Tempera paint (various colors) and Mod Podge, or Jazz Gloss tempera paint
- Paintbrush (medium round)
- Painting placemat

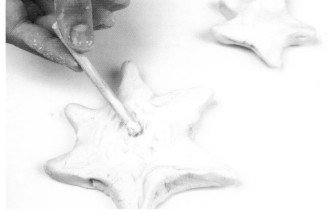

1. Start with a piece of 4" x 4" clay that is 1/2" thick. Cut the clay in half. Shape one of the pieces into a ball. Press it flat to the size of your palm and a thick pancake. Pinch sideways around the edge using your thumb and index finger to create petals. Split the second piece of clay in half. Set one of the pieces aside. Roll the other piece into a ball. Flatten and pinch the edges to create petals.

2. Take the larger piece of clay and roughen the surface by making little lines with the wooden stick. This is called scoring the clay. Spread some water on the score marks with your fingertip. This is called slip and acts as a glue for two pieces of clay to be stuck together. Place the second flattened piece of clay on top of the first, such that the petals are alternating. Repeat the score/ slip process on the top piece.

3. Roll the remaining piece of clay into a ball and press into the size of a silver dollar and place on top of the flower. Use the blunt end of the wooden stick to make indentations in this piece to represent the seeds. Let dry for three days, possibly more if you're in a humid climate.

4. Paint the sunflower with tempera paint or Jazz Gloss. Let dry overnight.

TIP: If you are using tempera paint and you'd like a shiny finish on your flower, add a coat of Mod Podge over the dried tempera paint. Be sure not to overwork the Mod Podge because it will reactivate the tempera paint.

ADDITIONAL ARTWORK

Still Life with Roses and Sunflowers (1886)

Branches with Almond Blossom (1890)

A Vase of Roses (1890)

FURTHER READING

Van Gogh and the Sunflowers (Anholt's Artists Books For Children) **by Laurence Anholt**

In the Garden with Van Gogh **by Julie Merberg and Suzanne Bober**

Vincent Van Gogh: Sunflowers and Swirly Stars (Smart About Art) **by Joan Holub**

MOUNTAIN LANDSCAPE

INSPIRED BY: *Mont Sainte-Victoire* (1902–1904) by Paul Cézanne
AGE: 7–12 years
PROJECT DURATION: 120 minutes plus overnight drying

ABOUT THE ARTIST

Paul Cézanne (January 19, 1839–October 22, 1906) was a French draftsman and painter, and one of the most influential artists in modern painting. He was a self-taught artist whose style and technique was considered odd, even by his fellow artists. Cézanne viewed nature as curved, as opposed to flat, so he used geometric shapes as the basis for his landscapes. And rather than use standard light and shade techniques, he placed different colors side by side to create a sense of depth. His methods were a huge influence on fellow artist Pablo Picasso and the Cubist style of art.

SUPPLIES

- Heavyweight drawing paper
- Permanent marker (black)
- Tempera paint
- Paintbrush (medium flat)
- Painting placemat
- Metallic oil pastels (optional)

1. Position the paper horizontally and use the permanent marker to draw a line across the middle of the paper. Draw a large mountain rising above the horizontal line (horizon line). Add a small building at the bottom of the paper in the foreground using simple geometric shapes such as a rectangle, square, parallelogram, and triangle. Add some lines on the mountain and in the middle ground to give some contour to the landscape.

2. Begin painting with light orange and yellow paint. Apply the paint in short squared brushstrokes to the building and below the horizon line. Make sure to overlap the brushstrokes. Some highlight strokes can be added to the mountain side as well.

3. Fill in the ground area with light green and medium green paint in squared brushstrokes. Alternate between overlapping vertical and horizontal brushstrokes. Once the ground is painted, add some trees out of darker shades of green and blue paint. To make the trees, gently dip your brush into the paint and dab at the bottom of the paper. You can also use turquoise and brown paint to create the illusion of different shades of trees. These irregular dabs will represent the forest.

4. Clean off any excess paint on your brush by wiping it on the placemat. If there's any paint left on the brush, that is OK because it will blend in with the other colors. Take the same process of painting that you used for the ground and apply that to the sky. Make squared brushstrokes in alternating vertical and horizontal directions using turquoise, blue, and a little white paint.

5. Use pink, peach, yellow, or purple paint, and apply it on top of the previously painted sky. Make sure not to over blend the sky colors, so you can see the variety of shades. This can be achieved by keeping the paint on the tip of the brush. With the white paint you can add some clouds and a snowcap on the mountain peak. Let dry overnight.

Option: Use dark blue and silver metallic oil pastels to create squared squiggles in the sky and to outline the mountain. Use green metallic oil pastels to highlight the right side of the trees and to create small squiggles on the ground. With gold or copper metallic oil pastels, add highlights to the building and the field. Using the metallic oil pastels adds an additional layer of interest to your painting.

ADDITIONAL ARTWORK

The Roofs (1876-1877)
Dish of Apples (1879)
Orchard (1882)

FURTHER READING

Cézanne and the Apple Boy (Anholt's Artists)
by Laurence Anholt
Paul Cézanne (Getting to Know the World's Greatest Artists)
by Mike Venezia
Paul Cézanne (Artists in Their Time) by Nathaniel Harris

ZINNIA STILL LIFE

INSPIRED BY: *Zinnias in a Blue Pot* by Clementine Hunter
AGE: 9–12 years
PROJECT DURATION: 95 minutes plus overnight drying

ABOUT THE ARTIST

Clementine Hunter (December 1886–January 1, 1988) was an African American folk artist from Louisiana. She lived and worked all her life on a plantation, first as a farm hand and later as a maid. A self-taught artist, Hunter is known for her bright and colorful paintings depicting plantation life in the early 1900s. She did not start painting until later in life and based her paintings on memories of the plantation. Her unique style is easily recognizable whether the subject is a funeral scene, cotton pickers working the fields, or a bowl of zinnias. Zinnias were her favorite flower and she would paint them every summer when in bloom. Due to unfair compensation for her labor, she could not afford any canvas to paint on, so Hunter would use non-traditional materials such as window shades, cardboard, paper bags, and unwanted fabrics. She is one of the Southern United States' most celebrated painters and greatest folk artists of all time.

SUPPLIES

- Construction paper (12" x 18" in various colors)
- Painted paper (bright colors for flowers)
- Tempera paint (one color of your choice for vase, light green, and dark green for stems and leaves, white for highlight)
- Paintbrush (medium round)
- Scissors
- Glue
- Pencil
- Painting placemat
- Circle template (optional)

1. Position the construction paper vertically. Paint a wide oval shape with a flat top and bottom as the base. If you want a handle on the vase, you can create a curving line like a backward letter "C."

2. Use both light and dark green paint to create flower stems by making gently curving lines extending from the top of the vase. Make leaves using shorter brushstrokes coming off the stems. Let dry overnight.

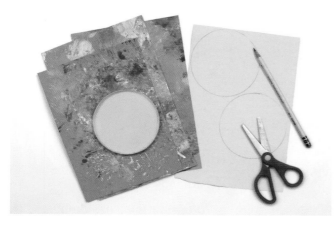

3. Make five to seven flowers out of painted paper. Use several colors of painted paper to add variety to the flowers. Draw the flowers in various sizes on the back of the paper. Drawing on the back side will prevent any pencil marks on the painted side once cut out. If needed, a circle template can be used. Add petals by drawing a gentle scalloped edge around the outside of each sketched circle. Cut out the flowers and glue them down on top of the green leaves such that the painted side of the flower is facing up.

4. Either cut out small circles from the leftover scraps of painted paper and glue them down in the center of the flowers or paint small circles in the center of the flowers.

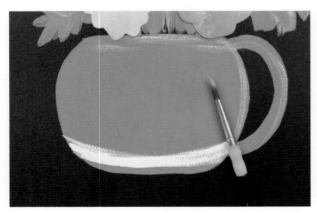

5. Use white paint to add a highlight along the bottom of the vase body. Let dry.

ADDITIONAL ARTWORK

Wash Day (1950)
Untitled (Dancing) (1965)
Two Women (1980–1986)

FURTHER READING

Talking With Tebe: Clementine Hunter, Memory Artist by Clementine Hunter and Mary E. Lyons
Art From Her Heart: Folk Artist Clementine Hunter by Kathy Whitehead

TOWERING TREES

INSPIRED BY: *Forest Landscape No. 2*. by Emily Carr
AGE: 9–12 years
PROJECT DURATION: 90 minutes

ABOUT THE ARTIST

Canadian-born Emily Carr (December 13, 1871–March 2, 1945) was a writer and painter from Victoria, British Columbia. Compared to the well-to-do Victorian society, Carr was an outspoken and independent person who considered herself an outcast. She could be seen around town pushing a beat-up stroller, loaded with dogs, cats, birds, and her favorite monkey Woo. Carr gained international attention at a time when women artists were ignored. Growing up in British Columbia, she was greatly influenced by the natural scenery of the Pacific Northwest and the First Nations people that lived there. She helped popularize the region and its people at a time when little was known of them outside the area. Her deep love and respect for the environment is apparent in her many landscapes of lush forests and towering trees. Today she is considered one of Canada's greatest artists, environmentalists, and icons.

SUPPLIES

- Cardboard or chipboard (7" x 9")
- Oil pastels
- Modeling clay

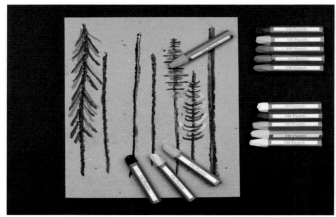
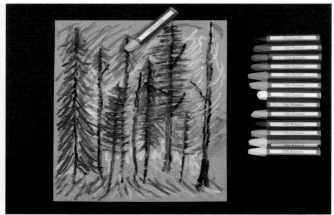

1. Position the cardboard vertically. Use black and brown oil pastels to draw six to eight tall, narrow tree trunks. Use gray oil pastel to add a highlight to one side of each trunk. Whichever side you highlight, do it on the same side of the others as well. Add different lengths of branches to each of the trees using a variety of shades of green oil pastels.

2. Put patches of color in the sky using different shades of blue oil pastels. Use yellow, tan, and brown oil pastels to create short, overlapping diagonal lines that represent the texture of the ground.

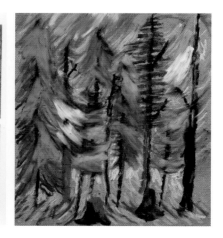

3. Use modeling clay to create a second layer on top of what you've already drawn. Take various shades of green clay, in small pieces, and lay them on top of the green branches. Use one finger to smear each piece of modeling clay. As soon as you begin to smear the clay with the oil pastel, it creates a blended, blurred effect in the style of Emily Carr's paintings. Repeat this process with white and shades of blue clay in the sky. Make rocks out of black, gray, and shades of brown clay at the base of the trees.

Option for Younger Artists

Draw basic tree shapes on cardboard. Fill in the shapes with tempera paint and let dry. Have an adult cut out the tree shapes. Stand the trees upright using modeling clay as a base.

ADDITIONAL ARTWORK

Chemainus Bay, Vancouver Island (1924–1925)

Church at Yuquot Village (1929)

Totem and Forest (1931)

FURTHER READING

When Emily Carr Met Woo by Monica Kulling

Emily Carr: At the Edge of the World by Jo Ellen Bogart

Emily Carr's Woo by Constance Horne

THE GREAT WAVE

INSPIRED BY: *The Great Wave Off Kanagawa* (1931) by Katsushika Hokusai

AGE: 7–12 years

PROJECT DURATION: 90 minutes plus overnight drying

ABOUT THE ARTIST

Katsushika Hokusai (October 30, 1760–May 10, 1849) was a Japanese artist born in what is now Tokyo, Japan. He was a painter and printmaker known mostly for his colored woodcut series titled *Thirty-Six Views of Mount Fuji*. The series was created over a seven-year period beginning in 1826. Each of the prints shows a different view of Mount Fuji at different times of the year. The first print of the series, and the most well known, is *The Great Wave Off Kanagawa*. The print shows a giant wave in the foreground that almost hides the volcanic mountain in the distance. This series of prints propelled Hokusai to widespread recognition and leaves a lasting impression on the art world to this day.

SUPPLIES

- Cardboard (4" x 6")
- One small package of air dry clay or Crayola's Model Magic
- Paintbrushes (medium round, large round, medium flat)
- Tempera paint (light blue, dark blue, peach, white, black)
- Tacky glue (use only if clay does not stick to cardboard)
- Painting placemat

1. Use a flat brush to paint the top half of the cardboard in a lighter color, such as peach blended with white. Paint the bottom half of the cardboard with black paint. Paint a small black mountain (Mount Fuji), on the lower right side of the cardboard. Use a clean flat paintbrush to paint the mountaintop white.

2. Create the large wave out of air dry clay. Form it in the shape of the letter "C." Add additional clay along the bottom to represent the smaller waves. Press the clay firmly to attach it to the cardboard. Be sure to leave the mountain visible behind the wave. Let dry overnight.

3. Use a medium round brush to paint the smaller waves and the underside of the large wave in light and dark blue tempera paint. Add white tempera paint to the top edges of the large wave and smaller waves.

4. Gently dip a large round brush into white paint. Lightly dab the paintbrush tips on the edges of the waves to create the look of spraying water.

Option for Younger Artists

Use gray or black crayon to shade the lower part of a tan piece of construction paper. Create the wave using dark blue tempera paint. Use the shape of the letter "C" as a guide to make the wave. On top of the dark blue, paint a lighter blue with a touch of white paint to complete the wave. Use a large round brush or foam brush to create the white caps on the waves.

ADDITIONAL ARTWORK

Cranes from Quick Lessons in Simplified Drawing (1823)
The Dragon of Smoke (undated)
Hibiscus and Sparrow (undated)

FURTHER READING

The Great Wave by Veronique Messenot
The Old Man Mad About Drawing: A Tale of Hokusai by Francois Place
Hokusai: The Man Who Painted a Mountain by Deborah Kogan Ray

WATER LILIES PAINTING

INSPIRED BY: *Water Lilies* series of paintings by Claude Monet
AGE: 9–12 years
PROJECT DURATION: 95 minutes

ABOUT THE ARTIST

Claude Monet (November 14, 1840–December 5, 1926) was a French painter and the Father of Impressionism, one of the most popular artistic movements of all time. He liked to paint outdoors in nature, a practice not previously possible due to the limitations of traditional art supplies. New art supplies however, such as paint in tubes, allowed artists to now take their supplies wherever they chose. By painting outdoors Monet could paint the same scene at different times of the day, enabling him to capture the changing color and light. Critics viewed this method as crude and impressionistic, giving the style its name. Monet was very fond of his home in Giverny, France. Its calm and peaceful garden with a pond, bridge, and water lilies was the subject of more than 250 of his outdoor paintings.

SUPPLIES

- Heavyweight drawing or watercolor paper
- Tempera paint (various colors)
- Paintbrushes (large flat, medium round)
- Painting placemat

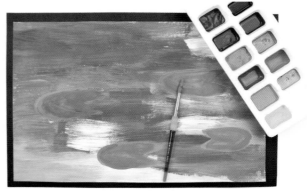

1. Painting the Water
   Position the paper horizontally. Choose three analogous colors. Analogous colors are colors next to each other on the color wheel. (Refer to the color wheel on page 10.) Magenta, purple, blue, green, turquoise, and yellow work well in the style that Monet painted. Use the large flat brush and paint large horizontal overlapping brushstrokes. Be careful not to over blend—you want the brushstrokes to be visible. To lighten your colors, add a touch of white to create a tint. Let dry.

2. Painting the Lily Pads
   With the medium round brush and shades of green paint, create three to five ovals with a triangular notch removed from one side. Fill in the oval with paint to make the lily pads. Wipe off the brush on the placemat.

3. Painting the Lily Flowers
   A. Choose a new color to make the first layer of petals. To create the shape of the lily flower, paint a gentle curved line that overlaps on the edge of the lily pad. The line should be in the shape of a small bowl or a semicircle. Add more petals by making short vertical brushstrokes inside the semicircle.
   B. Add a second layer of petals using the same steps as above; however, this time use a color analogous to the first layer (or create a new color by mixing a little white with the color used in the first layer). Be sure that your second layer of petals only slightly overlaps the first layer.
   C. Finally, make a third layer of petals using the same color as the first. Start at the bottom center of the flower and pull the brush upward, creating short strokes.

TIP: Keep the paint on the tip of your brush. You will have more control over your paint application, resulting in cleaner colors that are not so muddy.

ADDITIONAL ARTWORK

Impression, Sunrise (1873)

Antibes in the Morning (1888)

Waterloo Bridge, London (1903)

FURTHER READING

Claude Monet: Sunshine and Waterlilies (Smart About Art) by True Kelley

Claude Monet: Getting to Know the World's Greatest Artists by Mike Venezia

The Magical Garden of Claude Monet by Laurence Anholt

THISTLES IN THE WIND

INSPIRED BY: *Thistles* (1883–1889) by John Singer Sargent
AGE: 6–10 years
PROJECT DURATION: 90 minutes

ABOUT THE ARTIST

American painter John Singer Sargent (January 12, 1856–April 14, 1925) trained in Paris and lived in London. He was a citizen of the United States but did not visit the country until he was twenty years old. Sargent was a talented portrait painter and while in the United States he became well known for his portraits of high-society individuals. After a while, however, he became bored with portraits and began focusing on murals and landscapes. Inspired by his friendship with fellow painter Claude Monet, Sargent became interested in the Impressionist style of painting outdoors. Painting outdoors allowed him to capture the natural light and conditions at that specific moment. He eventually spent more time traveling, creating many landscapes using this open-air painting technique. Sargent's work fell out of fashion with the rise of modern art but has become popular again since the late 1900s.

SUPPLIES

- Watercolor paper
- Cardboard for paint scraper (3" x 1")
- Tempera paint (blue, burnt sienna, dark brown, white)
- Paint plate
- Paintbrush (large flat)
- Chalk pastels (warm colors)
- Painting placemat

1. Position the paper horizontally. Paint either a blue sky or a brown sky in the top third of the paper. Add some white paint to create a tint, making sure not to over blend the paints—you want to be able to see the various brushstrokes.

2. If you chose blue for your sky, use dark brown for your field; if you used brown for your sky, use gold/yellow for your field. As you add your field paint, create an irregular horizon line where the sky and field meet. Ultimately your painting should show more field than sky. Let dry overnight.

3. Take a lighter color of chalk pastel and lightly drag it across the field portion. Be sure not to color too hard so you can still see the paint color showing through. Use one finger to blend the chalk on the paper.

5. Dip the short edge of a piece of cardboard into white paint. Starting at the bottom of the paper, stamp a long stem. Stamp several shorter lines that connect back to this main stem at the top. Repeat this process across the paper. Stems can overlap each other like they are blowing in the wind.

4. Take a different color of chalk and make vertical and diagonal lines in the lower portion of the field. Gently blend the chalk using one finger.

TIP: Some of Sargent's thistle paintings have blue skies with dark brown fields, while others have brown skies with golden fields. Choose your color scheme, but the process will be the same.

ADDITIONAL ARTWORK

Claude Monet Painting by the Edge of a Wood (1885)

Mrs. Carl Meyer and Her Children (1896)

Venetian Canal (1913)

SEASCAPES

INSPIRED BY: *Eastern Point* (1900) by Winslow Homer
AGE: 5 years and up
PROJECT DURATION: 75 minutes

ABOUT THE ARTIST

Winslow Homer (February 24, 1836–September 29, 1910) was an American painter from Boston, Massachusetts. Many people consider him the greatest American painter of the nineteenth century. His passion was creating landscapes and marine-themed watercolor paintings. In 1859 he moved to New York City where he began working as a magazine illustrator reporting on the Civil War. Following the war he traveled extensively and began painting in watercolor. He eventually settled in Prout's Neck, Maine, where he focused solely on painting the struggles between man and nature. His many watercolor paintings during this period made Homer one of the best known painters of seascapes.

SUPPLIES

- Watercolor paper
- Tempera paint (various colors)
- Paintbrush (medium flat)
- Painting placemat

1. Create the sea and sky background by painting the entire watercolor paper with horizontal brushstrokes of shades of blue or shades of orange tempera paint. Adding a little white paint will create a tint. Clean any excess paint off your brush when finished.

2. Use white paint to add large puffy clouds to the previously painted sky. Use curving brushstrokes to create the appearance of movement in the clouds. Add a horizontal line of turquoise paint to the lower part of the paper to represent the sea. Add tan or orange paint across the entire bottom of the paper to represent the beach. Dab an irregular horizontal line of white paint where the sea and the beach meet.

3. Use black and shades of brown paint to add at least three or more large rocks. Place the rocks at the water's edge and at the lower part of the paper along the beach. Clean any excess paint off your brush. Add some white paint on the bottom of the rocks to represent splashing water. Let dry overnight.

ADDITIONAL ARTWORK

Snap the Whip (**1872**)

West Point, Prout's Neck (**1900**)

Summer Squall (**1904**)

FURTHER READING

Winslow Homer (Getting to Know the World's Greatest Artists) **by Mike Venezia**

FOLK ART FLOWERS

INSPIRED BY: Maud Lewis's painted house and the interior walls painted with flowers
AGE: 5-12 years
PROJECT DURATION: 90 minutes plus overnight drying

ABOUT THE ARTIST

Born in rural Nova Scotia, Canada, Maud Lewis (March 7, 1903–July 30, 1970) suffered from a series of birth defects that crippled her hands and left her hunched over, leaving her in excruciating pain. She lived her adult life in a one-room house with no electricity or running water. Despite these obstacles she earned a living for more than thirty years creating oil paintings on the most unusual surfaces such as cardboard, particleboard, and wallpaper. In addition to her physical disabilities, Lewis was incredibly shy, but she had a sweet personality and a charming smile for all who visited her brightly decorated home. She created hundreds of cheerful paintings in spite of her adversities, making her a folk art icon and an example of the triumph of the human spirit.

SUPPLIES

- Square piece of heavyweight drawing paper, tagboard, or poster board (using poster board will eliminate curling of the paper)

- Tempera paint (various colors)

- Paintbrush (medium round)

- Scissors

- Painting placemat

1. Paint a circle, approximately 3" in diameter, in the center of the paper or poster board. Use a different color to add large rounded petals around the circle.

2. Add patterns to your flowers. Simple designs work best. Outline the petals with a different color. Add details such as dots and dashes on top of the flower. Whatever pattern you create, repeat that around each petal. Let dry overnight.

3. Outline the shapes with black and white paint. Let dry overnight.

4. Cut out the flowers leaving a small border of unpainted white paper around the painted flower.

ADDITIONAL ARTWORK

White Cat Fluffy (1960)

Lighthouse. Yarmouth County (1965)

Deer (undated)

FURTHER READING

Maud Lewis 1, 2, 3 by Carol McDougall and Shanda LaRamee-Jones

Capturing Joy: The Story of Maud Lewis by Jo Ellen Bogart and Mark Lang

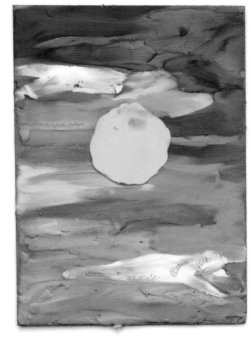
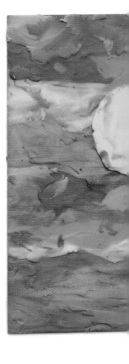
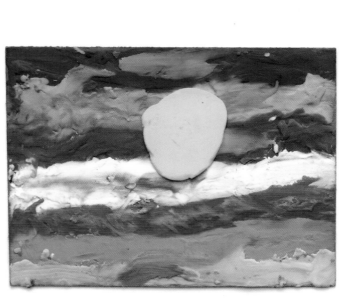

SETTING SUN OF COLORS

INSPIRED BY: *Landscape with Sun* (1909) by Max Ernst
AGE: 6 years and up
PROJECT DURATION: 60 minutes

ABOUT THE ARTIST

German-born Max Ernst (April 2, 1891–April 1, 1976) was a painter and sculptor who was interested in the thought process behind creativity. While studying psychology and psychiatry in school, he visited mental hospitals and was amazed by the art of the patients.

Ernst was very cautious of the modern world and did not like following directions. Instead, he enjoyed shocking people with his art and how it was created, employing various unique drawing processes and developing a technique used to create unusual textures and patterns in his art. This technique involved placing paper on an object and rubbing it with a pencil or crayon to transfer the image. The resulting patterns that were created intrigued Ernst and he enjoyed using them in his collage style paintings. His use of these processes were an important contribution to the Surrealist art movement.

SUPPLIES

- Cardboard or chipboard (4" x 6")
- Modeling clay (bright colors - no black)
- Mod Podge (optional)

1. Position the cardboard vertically. Start with a small chunk of modeling clay and make two stripes by pushing and smearing the clay across the bottom of the cardboard. Continue this process using other colors. Smearing the clay gently into the neighboring stripe will create interesting textures with the modeling clay. When finished, the entire cardboard should be covered with horizontal stripes of clay.

2. To create the sun, form a flattened circle out of the yellow clay. Place it on top of the first layer of modeling clay. Press the circle down to secure it in place.

TIP: Since modeling clay never dries out, applying a sealant such as Mod Podge will protect it.

Option for Younger Artists

Choose a piece of drawing paper for the background. Tear or cut irregular shapes out of painted paper. Look for colors that reflect the color wheel or rainbow colors. Glue down the irregular shapes in a rainbow pattern. Start at the bottom of the background paper and work upward. Add a sun in the center to complete your piece. Let dry.

ADDITIONAL ARTWORK

The Habit of Leaves (1925)

Red Forest (1970)

Configuration No. 6 (1974)

INTO THE WOODS

INSPIRED BY: *Wildboden Mountains Forest* (1927–1928) by Ernst Ludwig Kirchner
AGE: 9–12 years
PROJECT DURATION: 120 minutes plus overnight drying

ABOUT THE ARTIST

Ernst Ludwig Kirchner (May 6, 1880–June 15, 1938) was a German painter and printmaker known for his amazing woodcuts, engravings, and beautiful paintings of mountainous landscapes. He was a founding member of a group of German expressionist artists known as Die Brücke ("The Bridge"). He served as a soldier in World War I but left due to exhaustion. Upon his discharge from the army, he moved to Switzerland where he used art as a way to visually display his inner sadness after the war. He spent the rest of his life in Switzerland painting the rural scenery, villagers, and Swiss Alps. While gazing at the mountains at night, he was intrigued by the way the twilight twisted the colors and shapes of nature. Unfortunately, at the onset of World War II, local authorities labeled his (and the rest of the Die Brücke artists') artwork as gross and ugly because it wasn't like the traditional paintings that were popular at the time. All of it was banned and removed from their museums, leaving Kirchner heartbroken.

SUPPLIES

- Heavyweight drawing paper
- Tempera paint (various colors)
- Paintbrush (medium round)
- Pencil
- Oil pastels
- Painting placemat

1. Drawing
   A. Position the paper vertically. With a pencil, draw three to four tall trees that fill up the majority of the paper. For a more interesting look, draw the outer trees as pine trees with curvy branches that flare out. Make the middle tree an oblong shape like a long oval. Draw a trunk on each tree. Make the trunks go from the top of the tree all the way to the ground. The trees can be more abstract and organic in shape.
   B. Draw a horizon line where the sky and ground meet. The line should go across the paper but not intersect the trunks of the trees.
   C. Start at the horizon line and draw a winding path that gradually gets wider toward the bottom of the paper.

2. Sky
   Fill in areas of the sky with small patches of magenta (pink) paint. Make a tint of the magenta by mixing in a little white paint. Apply this light magenta or pink color to the remaining areas of the background. Use these same colors to fill in the path. As an option you can use pastel colors such as orange, peach, or yellow toward the horizon line. Let dry overnight.

3. Trees
   A. With a clean brush, paint the trees using various shades of green. Start with the lightest shade first and fill in the entire tree. Add some medium and dark greens to the tips of the branches. Overlap the colors and brushstrokes. Using the different shades of green will create more detail and add more interest to your painting.
   TIP: Dark green can be made by mixing green with a little bit of blue and black. Olive green can be made by mixing green with a little bit of brown.
   B. Paint the tree trunks with a turquoise or medium blue. Use the same blue to add some hills along the horizon line and clouds in the sky. Clean your brush on the placemat.
   C. Use light and medium green to add another layer of brushstrokes to the tree branches. This will represent the texture of the trees. Along the bottom of the painting and the base of the trees, use light green and yellow to create short vertical brushstrokes. These brushstrokes represent the patches of grass. Let dry overnight.

4. Oil Pastel Detail

Use short lines of various shades of green oil pastels to add texture and color to the tree branches. On the left-hand side of each tree trunk, use a dark blue oil pastel to add a shadow effect. You could also use oil pastels to create flowers in the field, small houses in the back-ground, and to outline the path and clouds.

ADDITIONAL ARTWORK

Winter Landscape in Moonlight (1919)

Blick auf Davos (1924)

View of Basel and the Rhine (1927-1928)

FURTHER READING

Ernst Ludwig Kirchner: Imaginary Travels by Wolfgang Henze, Lucius Grisebach, Thomas Roske, and Thorsten Sadowsky

TISSUE PETAL SUNFLOWERS

INSPIRED BY: *Sunflowers* (1932) by Emil Nolde
AGE: 7–12 years
PROJECT DURATION: 95 minutes plus overnight drying

ABOUT THE ARTIST

Emil Nolde (August 7, 1867–April 13, 1956) was an oil and watercolor painter from Germany. Born Emil Hansen into a family of farmers, he took the last name Nolde from a town near his birthplace. Nolde was expected to join the family farm but instead became a furniture carver and painter. He was a very religious person and, beginning in 1909 until his death, he painted over fifty religious themed pieces. His flower and landscape watercolors best display his spirituality. Nolde's success as an artist was cut short prior to World War II when local leaders labeled his art as disgraceful because he was outspoken against the political powers at the time. They removed it from their museums and instructed him not to paint. He refused and continued painting in secret using watercolor, which was easier to conceal. His vibrant flower-themed watercolor paintings are seen as a symbol of resistance against those who made him feel not worthy as a person and an artist.

SUPPLIES

- Heavyweight drawing paper
- Tempera paint (various colors)
- Paintbrush (medium flat)
- Tissue paper (yellow)
- Glue (sponges)
- Painting placemat

1. To create the sunflowers paint a circle and an oval, one lower and one higher, on the white paper. Make the edges of both jagged to represent the petals. Paint both shapes yellow first, then add an additional layer of yellow-orange paint on the edges of the petals. Be sure to show your brushstrokes and not over blend the colors. Clean off your brush on the placemat.

2. Add a dark green stem to both flowers. Paint large, light green, triangular leaves around the bottom of the flowers. Paint the tips of the leaves a light blue. Blend a touch of white into the blue to create a tint and a highlight. Do not over blend the colors to keep your brushstrokes visible. Clean off your brush.

3. Paint around the lower flower with a very light blue color. Continue painting the rest of the background with a darker blue such that the blues blend from light at the bottom to dark at the top.

4. Paint the centers of the sunflowers with brown and a touch of black. Gently hopping your brush around will give more texture to the center of the flowers. Clean off your brush on the placemat. If any brown paint is left on the brush, gently brush the excess paint at the top of the paper in the dark blue background. Let dry overnight.

5. Crumple small pieces of yellow and yellow-orange tissue paper. Tap the tissue onto the glue sponges. Glue the tissue down on the petal area of the flowers to create a three-dimensional effect.

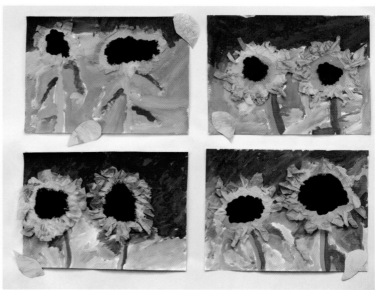

ADDITIONAL ARTWORK

Bay (1914)

Flower Garden (1919)

Colored Sky Above Marais (1940)

LAKE GEORGE LANDSCAPE

INSPIRED BY: *Lake George, Autumn* (1927) by Georgia O'Keeffe
AGE: 9–12 years
PROJECT DURATION: 90 minutes plus overnight drying

ABOUT THE ARTIST

Georgia O'Keeffe (November 15, 1887–March 6, 1986) was one of America's leading and most prolific artists, creating more than two thousand drawings, sculptures, and paintings throughout her life. She is known for painting a variety of works ranging from abstract swirling colors to highly detailed leaf and animal bone renderings. O'Keeffe also created various landscape paintings, both desert and forest. She grew up working on the family farm in Sun Prairie, Wisconsin, but also spent many of her summers as a young woman on the shores of Lake George in upstate New York. She loved painting the beautiful forests, mountains, and water of Lake George. In addition to the numerous trees and seasonal colors that inspired her, the barns and sheds in the area reminded her of her childhood on the Wisconsin farm.

SUPPLIES

- Construction paper (12" x 18" in turquoise, dark blue, light blue)
- Tempera paint (various colors)
- Paintbrushes (large round, small round, large flat)
- Painting placemat

1. **Sky**

   Start with a 12" x 18" piece of blue or turquoise construction paper. Fold the paper in half horizontally to create a central horizon line. Paint the sky area above the horizon line with a large flat brush and shades of light blue paint. Adding a little white paint while the sky paint is still wet will create various tints of the base color. Include some white clouds as well.

2. **Water**

   Using the same brush, paint the water below the horizon line with a dark shade of blue. Only paint to approximately 3" above the bottom of the paper. Wipe any excess paint on the brush onto the placemat.

3. **Mountains**

   With the large flat brush, paint mountains in the background with dark brown, light brown, and a terracotta color. A terracotta color can be achieved by mixing yellow and orange with brown. Don't over blend the paint and brushstrokes. Let dry overnight.

4. **Trees**

   A. At the base of the mountains, paint small trees. Use a large round brush with various shades of yellow, orange, red, and light brown. Paint the colors in that order to keep your colors from becoming muddy. Also, keep the paint on the tip of your brush and hop the brush around while shaping your trees. Hopping the brush will create a texture and more realistic looking trees.

   B. Repeat this process at the bottom of the paper in the foreground, making larger, overlapping, oval-shaped trees. The items in the foreground will be the largest since they are the closest to you.

5. Gently dip the tip of a small round brush into black or brown paint. On the trees in the foreground, create simple vertical lines to represent the trunks. Add smaller angled strokes off the trunks to represent the branches.

Option for Younger Artists

Choose a warm color piece of painted paper. Trace a large leaf shape on the back side of the paper. Cut out the leaf and paint veins with dark brown tempera paint. Outline the edge of the leaf with the brown paint. Let dry.

ADDITIONAL ARTWORK

Evening Star IV (1917)
Oriental Poppies (1927)
Chama River, Ghost Ranch (1937)

FURTHER READING

My Name is Georgia by Jeanette Winter
Georgia O'Keeffe (Getting to Know the World's Greatest Artists) by Mike Venezia
Georgia O'Keeffe: Portraits of Women Artists for Children by Robyn Montana Turner
Through Georgia's Eyes by Rachel Victoria Rodriguez and Julie Paschkis

POLKA DOT PUMPKINS

INSPIRED BY: *Yayoi Kusama: All the Eternal Love I Have for the Pumpkins* (2016),
an Infinity Mirror Room Installation by Yayoi Kusama
AGE: 7–12 years
PROJECT DURATION: 120 minutes plus 3 or more days of drying time

ABOUT THE ARTIST

Sometimes referred to as the "Queen of Polka Dots," Yayoi Kusama (March 22, 1929) is a Japanese avant-garde sculptor, painter, and writer. Her artwork is easily recognizable by its use of repeating dots, pumpkins, mushrooms, and mirrors. Kusama grew up in Japan and started painting at the age of ten. Around this time she began experiencing the bizarre hallucinations and dreamy visions that would follow her into adulthood and serve to fuel her creativity. At first her parents did not want her to become an artist, but eventually she convinced them to enroll her in art school where she studied painting. In the late 1950s she left Japan and traveled to the United States where she began associating with other avant-garde artists like Andy Warhol. She was influential to the Pop Art movement and became a major figure in the New York City art scene with her wildly imaginative creations.

SUPPLIES

- Air dry clay
- Wooden craft stick or Popsicle stick to cut the clay
- Cup of water
- Tempera paint (various colors) and Mod Podge, or Jazz Gloss tempera paint
- Paintbrushes (small round, medium flat)
- Rolling pin
- Brown paper lunch bag
- Painting placemat

1. Roll the clay into a medium-sized pancake, roughly 7" in diameter. Peel a little chunk of clay from the edge of the pancake and put aside to make the stem.

2. Crumple the lunch bag into a ball. This will become the form for the pumpkin. Gently wrap the flattened clay around the crumpled lunch bag. Leave the bottom exposed so that air can pass through.
TIP: Don't wrap the clay too tightly around the crumpled bag or the clay might crack.

3. Take the smaller piece of clay and gently roll it back and forth with your fingertips on a flat surface to make a coil or a snake shape. Use the tip of the wooden craft stick to make little score marks on the top center of the pumpkin. This is called scoring the clay. Spread some water on the score marks with your fingertip. This is called slip and acts as a glue for two pieces of clay to be stuck together. Attach the coil of clay to the score marks, curling the clay to make the stem. Take the end of a paintbrush and press it into the sides of the pumpkin to create the ridges down the sides.

4. Dip your fingertip in water and smooth out any cracks that you see in the clay. Make sure not to oversaturate the clay. Let dry for at least three days.

5. Paint the pumpkin one solid color. Let dry overnight. Use a contrasting color to paint dots between the ridges of the pumpkin by making a row of larger dots down the center surrounded by rows of smaller dots. Paint the stem the same color as the dots. Let dry overnight.

ADDITIONAL ARTWORK

Dress (1982)

Dandelions (1985)

Watching the Sea (1989)

FURTHER READING

Yayoi Kusama From Here to Eternity by Sarah Suzuki and Ellen Weinstein

REFLECTIONS OF THE SUN

INSPIRED BY: *Without Borders* (2011) by Peter Max
AGE: 9–12 years
PROJECT DURATION: 90 minutes plus overnight drying

ABOUT THE ARTIST

German-born artist Peter Max (October 19, 1937) came to prominence during the psychedelic and Pop Art periods of 1960s America. He and his parents immigrated to the United States in the early 1950s and settled in Brooklyn, New York. Max got his start working in commercial art and graphic design. His cosmic elements and vibrant bursts of rainbow colors became associated with the 1960s counterculture, and items such as pop music album covers and tour posters. Max's distinctly recognizable style became so popular, it landed him on the cover of Life Magazine in 1969. In more recent years he has continued his colorful creations, focusing on American symbols like the nation's flag and the Statue of Liberty, as a reflection of his love and appreciation for his adoptive country.

SUPPLIES

- Heavyweight drawing paper (9" x 12")
- Tempera paint (various colors)
- Paintbrush (medium flat)
- Painting placemat
- Circle template or small paper plate (optional)

Peter Max is known for the broad brushstrokes in his later paintings, so make sure not to over blend the paint colors to keep your brushstrokes visible. To help control the paint, keep the paint on the tip of your brush to avoid saturating the bristles. This will help when you clean your brush on your placemat in between color changes and will conserve paint.

1. Position the paper horizontally. Create a circle for the sun by tracing around a circle template, small paper plate, or drawing by freehand. Paint the entire sun yellow. Mix in a little orange in the middle and red on the outer edge. Use the same three colors to create an irregularly shaped reflection underneath the sun.

2. Add the hills at the bottom of the paper on both sides of the reflection. Create the hills by making gentle, curved brushstrokes using yellow, blue, and different shades of green paint.

3. Use blue and turquoise to paint the sky around the sun, and the water around the reflection.

4. While the paint is still wet, blend some white in around the sun and in the water. Let dry overnight.

5. To create clouds, use curved brushstrokes and white paint. Keep the clouds to the sides of the sun. Also add white in the water along the edge of the reflection.

6. To create trees on the hills, make small paint dabs in various shades of blue and green, with brown vertical lines for trunks.

ADDITIONAL ARTWORK

Love (1969)

Liberty Head (1986)

Flag with Heart (1999)

ALFALFA FIELDS

INSPIRED BY: *Alfalfa, St. Denis* (1885-1886) by Georges Seurat
AGE: 5-8 years
PROJECT DURATION: 60 minutes

ABOUT THE ARTIST

Georges Seurat (December 2, 1859-March 29, 1891) was a French draftsman and painter who was interested in the science behind art. He produced many paintings using a technique he founded called pointillism, in which tiny, contrasting dots of color are placed side by side on the canvas. Up close the painting appears as individual dots, but when viewed from a distance the eye mixes the colors into a whole scene. His masterpiece, *Sunday Afternoon on the Island of La Grande Jatte*, is a huge work painted entirely using this method. Along with pointillism, Seurat's experimentation with color theory brought new ideas and concepts to the art world. He felt color could create harmony and emotion in painting similar to how a musician creates harmony in music.

SUPPLIES

- Heavyweight drawing paper
- Tempera paint (yellow, orange, white, light green, dark green)
- Paintbrush (large round)
- Painting placemat

1. Sky

A. Position the paper horizontally. Create a sky in the top third of the paper using yellow, white, and a touch of light green paint. Use light green to create a horizon line below the sky. Create a horizon line of overlapping circles by holding the brush vertically and stamping straight down repeatedly as you move across the page.

2. Field

A. Repeat the stamping process along the bottom third of the paper using gradually darker green paints. While the dark green paint is still wet, tap your brush into yellow paint and overlap some dots into the green. This will create various tints. Make sure to add white if you want a lighter color, and dark green in areas where you want the field to be darker.

B. Lightly tap a little orange paint in the middle of the field, closer to the horizon line. This will represent small flowers in the distance. Make sure to add a little bit of yellow and green on top of the orange, but don't cover the orange completely. Hopping your brush around will create the dots that Seurat is so well known for.

Option for Younger Artists

Position a 9" x 12" piece of heavyweight drawing paper horizontally. Start with a yellow paint dauber and dot across the paper approximately 3" from the top of the paper. Use green and teal daubers to add dots down to the bottom of the paper, being sure to overlap on top of the yellow dots. Use a brown dauber to add a few dots across the bottom of the paper on top of the green dots. Use an orange dauber to place a couple patches of dots where the yellow and green meet.

ADDITIONAL ARTWORK

The Watering Can (1883)

Sunday Afternoon on the Island of La Grande Jatte (1884)

The Eiffel Tower (1889)

FURTHER READING

Georges Seurat (Getting to Know the World's Greatest Artists) by Mike Venezia

Sunday with Seurat (Mini Masters) by Julie Merberg and Suzanne Bober

Seurat and La Grande Jatte: Connecting the Dots by Robert Burleigh

FLOWER BOUQUET

INSPIRED BY: *Roses* (1894) by Berthe Morisot
AGE: 8–13 years
PROJECT DURATION: 90 minutes

ABOUT THE ARTIST

Painter Berthe Morisot (January 14, 1841–March 2, 1895) was born in Bourges, France, and dreamt of becoming an artist from an early age. Her mother supported her daughter's dreams by making sure she had the best art education. Morisot excelled artistically not only due to her talent but also the encouragement of her family to follow her dreams. She would frequent the Louvre in Paris, and copy paintings created by master artists. She also developed a love for landscape, portraits, and still-life painting. Morisot cultivated her artistic talents and achieved success at an early age with acceptance to the Paris Salon at age twenty-three. In 1874, she was invited to exhibit with the first exhibition of the Impressionists. Her art was often overlooked, however, due to its feminine qualities such as her use of spontaneous and delicate brushstrokes. As a woman Morisot was often discriminated against and was not allowed in many of the places her male friends frequented. That did not stop her drive to become an artist, and for more than three decades she created paintings that have helped guide the direction of French art.

SUPPLIES

- Construction paper (square)
- Tempera paint (various colors)
- Paintbrushes (medium round, small flat)
- Painting placemat

1. Use black tempera paint and a medium round brush to create a large round vase on the colored construction paper. To help visualize the size of the vase, I suggest that students place their hand on the paper as a reference. At the top of the vase, add five to six circle shapes for flowers. Put dots in the center of each circle. Add a few leaves among the flowers. Paint a horizontal line across the paper approximately halfway up from the bottom edge. This line is the edge of the table. Make sure to keep the line on the outside of the vase. Do not paint across the vase.

2. Clean any excess black paint off the brush by wiping it in the tabletop area of the construction paper. Use a small flat brush to mix white tempera paint with the black, creating a gray shade. Fill in the tabletop. Make sure not to add too much white. This will help the background paper color show through.

3. Continue with the small flat brush. Paint the flowers using bright, warm colors such as yellow, orange, and magenta, starting with the lightest color first. Make sure to overlap your brushstrokes in a circular motion. Add a small amount of white paint to the colors to create various tints of the original colors. Be sure not to over mix the paint. Wipe any excess paint off the brush onto the paper above the table line. This will establish the wall color.

4. Continue with the small flat brush. Paint the leaves green, starting with light green and finishing with dark green. Add a few flat brushstrokes to represent longer leaves in the background. Choose one color for the vase and fill in with short, overlapping brushstrokes. Add some white to create a tint but don't over blend the colors.

ADDITIONAL ARTWORK

The Cradle (1872)
The Cage (1885)
The Goose (1885)

THE STARRY NIGHT

INSPIRED BY: *The Starry Night* (1889) by Vincent Van Gogh
AGE: 9–13 years
PROJECT DURATION: 90 minutes

ABOUT THE ARTIST

Vincent Van Gogh (March 30, 1853–July 29, 1890) was a Dutch painter and one of the most well-known artists in the world. Many people of his time found his behavior eccentric, isolating Van Gogh and creating a difficult life for him. Since people didn't understand him, he unsuccessfully held many jobs until age twenty-seven when he decided to become a painter. He loved nature and began his career painting countryside landscapes. After he moved to Paris he started producing colorful flower still lifes and self-portraits. Van Gogh liked working with bold colors and applied his paint in thick layers, often directly from the tube. The thick paint and visible brushstrokes give the surface of his paintings a bumpy appearance. Van Gogh was virtually unknown in his time. Some accounts even say he sold only one painting during his lifetime. Today his life and work are world famous and his influences are reflected in many art movements.

SUPPLIES

- Heavyweight drawing paper (9" x 12")
- Tempera paint (various colors)
- Paintbrush (medium round)
- Pencil
- Painting placemat

1. To ensure a successful project, first draw out your starry night on the white drawing paper. Create a moon, cypress tree, hills, swirls in the sky, and a small town.

2. Start with the lightest color tempera paint and fill in the moon and stars. Make sure not to over blend the brushstrokes. Paint the windows of the town buildings yellow.

3. Use various shades of blue to create swirls around the stars in the sky. Add white if lighter shades of blue are desired.

4. Paint the hills and ground with darker shades of blue and green. Paint the small town with white paint and a touch of purple. Apply brown and orange paint to the cypress tree and edge of the hills. Outline the town with purple or blue paint.

ADDITIONAL ARTWORK

The Potato Eaters (1885)

Café Terrace at Night (1888)

The Bedroom (1889)

FURTHER READING

Vincent Van Gogh (Getting to Know the World's Greatest Artists) **by Mike Venezia**

Vincent, Theo and the Fox: A mischievous adventure through the paintings of Vincent Van Gogh (Artist Adventures Book 1) **by Ted Macaluso and Vincent van Gogh**

Van Gogh: Explore Vincent Van Gogh's Life and Art, and the Influences That Shaped His Work (DK Eyewitness Books) **by Bruce Bernard and Phil Hunt**

Vincent Can't Sleep: Van Gogh Paints the Night Sky **by Barb Rosenstock and Mary GrandPré**

SPOTTED MUSHROOMS

INSPIRED BY: *Mushrooms* (1995) by Yayoi Kusama
AGE: 9–12 years
PROJECT DURATION: 90 minutes plus overnight drying

ABOUT THE ARTIST

Sometimes referred to as the "Queen of Polka Dots," Yayoi Kusama (March 22, 1929) is a Japanese avant-garde sculptor, painter, and writer. Her artwork is easily recognizable by its use of repeating dots, pumpkins, mushrooms, and mirrors. Kusama grew up in Japan and started painting at the age of ten. Around this time she began experiencing the bizarre hallucinations and dreamy visions that would follow her into adulthood and serve to fuel her creativity. At first her parents did not want her to become an artist but eventually she convinced them to enroll her in art school where she studied painting. In the late 1950s she left Japan and traveled to the United States where she began associating with other avant-garde artists like Andy Warhol. She was influential to the Pop Art movement and became a major figure in the New York City art scene with her wildly imaginative creations.

SUPPLIES

- Construction paper or painted paper (various colors)
- Tempera paint (various colors)
- Paintbrushes (small round, medium round, large round, large flat)
- Small bubble wrap
- Painting placemat

1. Use a piece of previously painted paper or construction paper for the background. Place the bubble wrap with the bubbles facing up. Paint over the bubbles using a large flat brush and up to two analogous colors. Analogous colors are colors next to each other on the color wheel. (Refer to the color wheel on page 10.) Flip the bubble wrap over onto the background paper and gently rub the bubble wrap to transfer the paint, creating a polka dotted pattern. Be sure the pattern fills the entire paper all the way to the edges. Let dry for ten minutes.

   TIP: For an easy transfer, cut the bubble wrap the same size as the background paper.

2. Use the medium and large round brushes to paint various sizes of mushroom tops and stems on the background. If you prefer, draw the mushrooms in pencil prior to painting. The mushroom tops should be rounded or bell shaped. The stems should be at least the thickness of your finger. Create a total of five to seven mushrooms. If using black paint, make sure it is done last so your colors do not get muddy. Let dry overnight.

3. Add various dots to the mushroom tops and stems. Use small and medium round brushes and contrasting colors of paint. The contrasting colors will make the dots standout.

   TIP: To paint like Kusama, have larger dots in the middle of the stems and smaller dots along the edges.

ADDITIONAL ARTWORK

Flowers (1983)

Shoes (1985)

Ready to Blossom in the Morning (1989)

FURTHER READING

Yayoi Kusama From Here to Eternity
by Sarah Suzuki and Ellen Weinstein

WATER LILY CLAY SCULPTURE

INSPIRED BY: *Water Lilies series of paintings* by Claude Monet
AGE: 8–12 years
PROJECT DURATION: 95 minutes plus overnight drying

ABOUT THE ARTIST

Claude Monet (November 14, 1840–December 5, 1926) was a French painter and the Father of Impressionism, one of the most popular artistic movements of all time. He liked to paint outdoors in nature, a practice not previously possible due to the limitations of traditional art supplies. In 1883 Monet moved to Giverny, France, where he focused on nature and the various conditions of natural light. In his later years he never left his home in Giverny. He designed his gardens, including a pond filled with water lilies, which inspired him for the remainder of his life.

SUPPLIES

- Air dry clay
- Wooden craft stick or Popsicle stick
- Cup of water
- Tempera paint (various colors) and Mod Podge, or Jazz Gloss tempera paint
- Paintbrush (medium round)
- Painting placemat

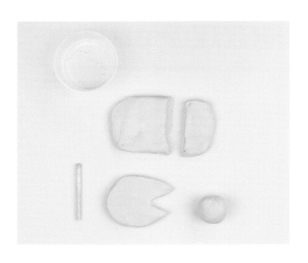

1. Preparing the Clay
   A. Divide a square slab of clay into two pieces. Make sure one is bigger than the other. The bigger piece will become the lily pad and the smaller piece the flower. Roll the bigger piece into a ball with the palms of your hands. Press it flat with your hand to create an oval shape. Make sure it's about the thickness of a pancake. Cut a triangle wedge out of the end of the oval with the wooden skewer.

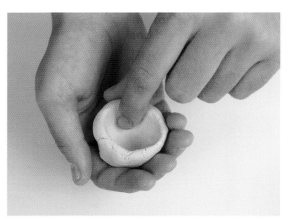

2. Forming the Flower
   A. Roll the smaller piece of clay into a ball. Put the ball into the palm of your non-writing hand. Use your index finger to push into the ball, being careful not to push all the way through. You will be making a small pinch pot. Use your thumb and index finger to pinch around the edge to open up the ball, creating a small bowl.

   B. Pinch and pull around the edge of the bowl to remove some of the clay, creating the petals of the flower. Shape the petals if needed. Roll two pieces of clay into the shape of two worms. Gently curve the worms into two letter "U"s. With your fingertip, apply a small amount of water in the bowl (flower). This is called slip and acts as a glue for two pieces of clay to be stuck together. Insert the two "U"s into the bowl to form the inside details of the flower.

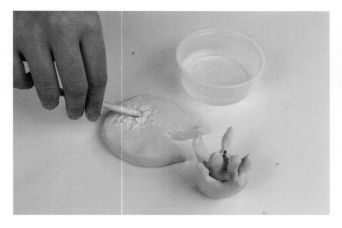 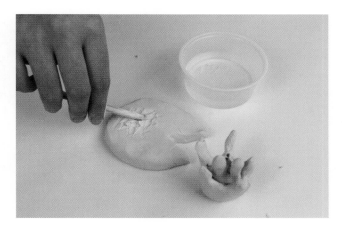

3. Assembling the Flower and Lily Pad
   A. Score the top of the oval-shaped clay (lily pad) with the wooden skewer. Spread some water on the score marks with your fingertip.

   B. Attach the flower to the scored area of the lily pad. Smooth out the clay where they connect. Use the skewer to create veins on the lily pad. Make sure not to push too hard. Let dry for a couple days.

4. Painting
   A. Paint the lily pad and flower with tempera paint or Jazz Gloss. Let dry overnight.

TIP: If you are using tempera paint and you want a shiny finish on your lily pad and flower, add a coat of Mod Podge over the dried tempera paint. Be sure not to overwork the Mod Podge because it will reactivate the tempera paint.

ADDITIONAL ARTWORK

The Artist's Garden at Vétheuil (1880)
Water Lilies and Japanese Bridge (1899)
San Giorgio Maggiore at Dusk (1912)

FURTHER READING

Linnea in Monet's Garden by Christina Björk, Lena Anderson, and Joan Sandin
A Picnic with Monet (Mini Masters) by Julie Merberg and Suzanne Bober
Who Was Claude Monet? by Ann Waldron and Nancy Harrison

DAZZLING LANDSCAPES WITH PATTERNED TREES

INSPIRED BY: *Landscape with Tree* (2012) by Mickalene Thomas

AGE: 9-12 years

PROJECT DURATION: 120 minutes plus overnight drying

ABOUT THE ARTIST

Mickalene Thomas (January 28, 1971) is an African American artist based in Brooklyn, New York. She is best known for painting elaborate portraits of African American women that explore the issues of femininity, race, and beauty. Her work is a combination of pop culture and art history influences. More recently she has begun focusing on landscapes inspired in part by her extensive travels. For Thomas, landscapes are an extension of the body, of nature and beauty. Central to her paintings is the use of colorful acrylic paints and rhinestones, her signature materials.

SUPPLIES

- Heavyweight drawing paper
- Patterned paper scraps (construction paper, painted paper, origami paper, magazine pages)
- Glue
- Scissors
- Glitter
- Sequins

1. Use various shapes of blue scrap paper to create the sky. Glue them down on the top half of the paper, overlapping as necessary to make sure that there is no white paper showing through.

2. Next create the ground using various shapes of green scrap paper. Glue them down on the bottom half of the paper, overlapping as necessary to make sure that there is no white paper showing through.

3. Add landscape details such as trees, plants, rocks, clouds, and sun made from scrap paper. Use colors that will stand out from the blue and green background. Glue them all down on the background.

4. Glue sequins and glitter to the tree foliage, bark, and plants on the ground. Let dry overnight.

ADDITIONAL ARTWORK

Something You Can Feel (2008)

Michelle Obama (2008)

Interior: Two Chairs and a Fireplace (2011)

HEART

INSPIRED BY: *The Confetti Heart* (1985) by Jim Dine
AGE: 9–12 years
PROJECT DURATION: 90 minutes plus overnight drying

ABOUT THE ARTIST

Jim Dine (June 16, 1935) is a painter, sculptor, printmaker, illustrator, performance artist, and poet from Cincinnati, Ohio. In 1958 he moved to New York City and opened a small theatre known as Happenings. Happenings were groundbreaking theatrical events involving spontaneous productions and audience participation staged in disorderly, improvised environments. By the early 1960s Dine began focusing on painting, particularly common everyday objects such as clothing, tools, and household items. One item he is best known for painting is a men's bathrobe. Another of his favorite shapes to paint is a heart. The heart is a very personal image he uses to represent his thoughts and emotions. He usually paints them in a vibrant patchwork of colors, often repeating the shape more than once in a painting.

SUPPLIES

- Heavyweight drawing paper (large square)
- Tempera paint (various colors)
- Paintbrush (medium round)
- Painting placemat
- Pencil (optional)

1. Paint a heart in the center of the paper. As an option, the heart can be drawn in pencil first. Use various colors of paint to fill in the heart. Start with the lightest color and work toward the darkest. Avoid over blending the colors to ensure your brushstrokes are visible.

2. With a clean brush start creating a patchwork look by painting brushstrokes in the background area of the paper around the heart. Start with the lightest color first and paint a few random brushstrokes. Continue this process as you work through your colors from lightest to darkest. When moving on to the next color, clean off your brush by wiping it on the edge of the placemat. Paint a white border along the edge of the paper. Paint a black border next to the white, being sure to slightly overlap the two colors. Gently outline the heart with a little bit of black paint. Let dry overnight.

ADDITIONAL ARTWORK

Four Hearts (1969)

Big Red Wrench in Landscape (1973)

The Robe (1985)

COKE BOTTLE

INSPIRED BY: *Coca-Cola Bottles* by Howard Finster
AGE: 8–12 years
PROJECT DURATION: 60 minutes plus overnight drying

ABOUT THE ARTIST

Howard Finster (December 2, 1916–October 22, 2001) was an American folk artist and minister originally from Valley Head, Alabama. One of thirteen children, he attended school until the sixth grade only. Finster was a self-taught artist whose inspiration came mostly from spiritual visions. He is known for his unusual paintings and sculptures that are covered with biblical verses. Combining his religious message with pop culture icons was a tool to aid in spreading his message. One such icon, the Coca-Cola bottle, was a recurring element in much of his work. He was fond of the famous contoured bottle and often decorated it with cloud, rainbow, and cross designs. As part of a global art project, Finster was hired by the Coca-Cola Company to create an eight-foot tall bottle for display at the 1996 Olympic Games in Atlanta, Georgia.

SUPPLIES

- Cardboard or chipboard (rectangle)
- Sequins
- Tacky glue
- Scissors
- Pencil
- Tempera paint (white)
- Paintbrush (medium round)
- Permanent marker (black)
- Markers (various colors)
- Painting placemat

1. Draw a Coke bottle in pencil on the cardboard. Paint the bottle white with a thick enough coat of paint that the cardboard does not show through. Let dry overnight.

2. In pencil, sketch out designs on the bottle. Simple designs Finster is known for are clouds, rainbows, flowers, hearts, crosses, angels, and smiling faces. Don't forget to add the name Coca-Cola!

3. Color in your designs using markers, but leave the background white. Use black permanent marker to outline the bottle and all of the designs.
   TIP: If markers pick up the white paint on their tips, use the edge of the cardboard to clean off the paint.

4. Cut out the bottle, leaving a border of cardboard around the edge. To stand the bottle up to display it, tape a piece of scrap cardboard to the back at a right angle near the bottom as a support.

ADDITIONAL ARTWORK

Paradise Gardens, Summerville, GA

George Washington at 23 (1992)

If A Shoe Fits, Wear It (1995)

FURTHER READING

Paradise Garden by Robert Peacock

QUILTS

INSPIRED BY: *The Quilts of Gee's Bend*
AGE: 5-10 years
PROJECT DURATION: 90 minutes

ABOUT THE ARTIST

Gee's Bend is a small, remote African American community in Alabama, surrounded on three sides by the Alabama River. There are roughly seven hundred residents of this rural area, mostly descendants of enslaved people. Since the early 1800s the women of Gee's Bend have produced hundreds of handmade quilts, often recycling old clothes and textiles to use as their fabric. Originally the bits of cloth were pieced together to make bed coverings. In later years, the tradition continued out of necessity to keep their families warm in their unheated homes, which cruelly lacked electricity or running water. Over time these remarkable quilts gained attention for their unique yet simple style, characterized by nontraditional patterns and unusual colors. These amazing tapestries hold an important place in the history of African American art and civil rights.

SUPPLIES

- Construction paper squares (shades of blue)
- Blue jean strips, blue fabric scraps, and/or patterned blue scrapbook paper
- Painted paper (shades of blue)
- Scissors
- Glue
- Tempera paint (shades of blue)
- Paintbrush (medium flat)
- Ruler
- Pencil
- Painting placemat

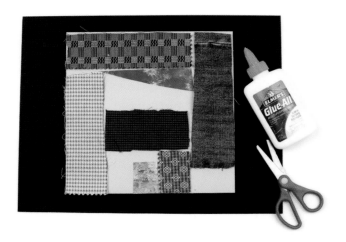

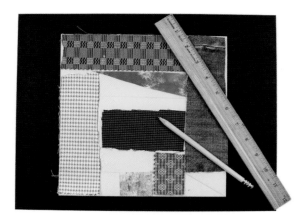

1. Cut strips of fabric to fit on a square of construction paper. Position the strips so they touch one another but do not overlap. Leave some open space for the painted paper. Cut painted paper into geometric shapes and position them among the fabric pieces. Leave some open space to paint. When you are happy with your layout, go ahead and glue down your pieces on the background paper.

2. Use a ruler to divide the open areas of background paper into basic shapes such as triangles, rectangles, and squares.

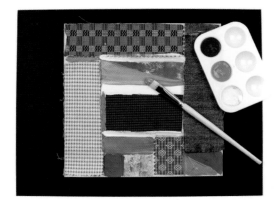

3. Fill in the open areas with shades of blue paint. Begin with the lightest color first and work through to the darkest color. Let dry.

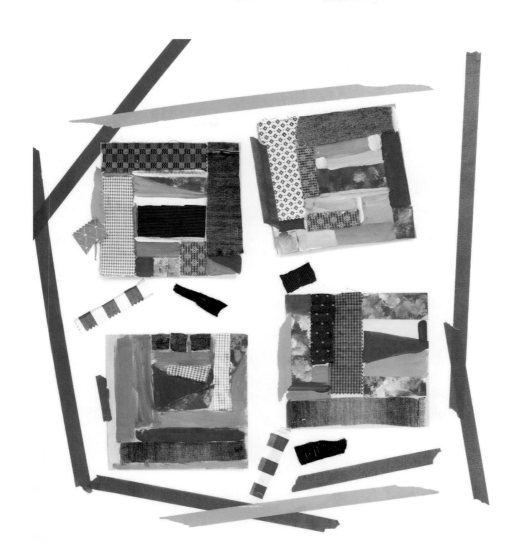

ADDITIONAL ARTWORK

Pig in the Pen
Housetop–Half-Log Cabin Variation (**1930s**)
Road to California (**1970**)

FURTHER READING

The Quilts of Gee's Bend **by Susan Goldman Rubin**
Stitchin' and Pullin': A Gee's Bend Quilt **by Patricia McKissack**
Belle, The Last Mule at Gee's Bend: A Civil Rights Story
by Calvin Alexander Ramsey and Bettye Stroud

MUSIC AND MOVEMENT

INSPIRED BY: *Composition 1* (1996) by Roy Lichtenstein
AGE: 5–12 years
PROJECT DURATION: 60 minutes plus overnight drying

ABOUT THE ARTIST

American painter and printmaker Roy Lichtenstein (October 27, 1923–September 29, 1997) was one of the first artists from the Pop Art world to gain wide acclaim. Pop artists of the 1960s were inspired by various icons in American popular culture like television, cartoons, and celebrities. Roy was specifically interested in comic book and advertising images. He is best known for painting oversized, comic-book style pictures. Most of these paintings are created using only four colors, imitating the four ink colors that printers use. Another of Roy's signature techniques is reproducing the numerous tiny dots that make up a printed image, similar to that in newspaper printing. When viewed up close the individual dots are visible, but from a distance they form a complete image. In addition to art, Lichtenstein also loved music and played the flute and saxophone. He especially liked jazz music, which is based on improvisation.

SUPPLIES

- Heavyweight drawing paper
- Construction paper (yellow, red, blue)
- Permanent marker (black)
- Glue (sponge)
- Large flat paintbrush for painting on bubble wrap
- Tempera paint (red, white)
- Bubble wrap
- Paper plate
- Painting placemat

1. **Printing Dot Patterns on Paper**
   Use a piece of construction paper for the background. Place the bubble wrap with the bubbles facing up. Paint over the bubbles using a large flat brush and a contrasting color. Prints look best when the paint and paper are contrasting colors (for example, red paint on yellow paper, or white paint on blue or red paper). Flip the bubble wrap over onto the background paper and gently rub the bubble wrap to transfer the paint, creating a polka dotted pattern. Be sure the pattern fills the entire paper all the way to the edges. Repeat this process using different colors of paper and paint. Let dry overnight.
   TIP: For an easy transfer, cut the bubble wrap the same size as the background paper.

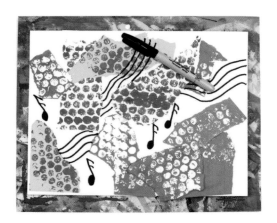

2. Tear the painted dot paper into different shapes and glue them down onto the white heavy-weight paper in a random pattern.

3. Use a black permanent marker to create at least three individual music staves with music notes, in separate locations on the paper. A musical stave is the set of five equally spaced horizontal lines on which musical notes are written. The horizontal lines do not have to be straight. They can be wavy or flowing. Draw music notes along the staves with black permanent marker.

ADDITIONAL ARTWORK

Kitchen Range (1961–1962)

Whaam! (1963)

Cape Cod Still Life (1972)

FURTHER READING

Roy Lichtenstein (Getting to Know the World's Greatest Artists) by Mike Venezia

Lichtenstein (Basic Art Series 2.0) by Janis Hendrickson

SPLASHES OF COLOR

INSPIRED BY: *Tutti-Frutti* (1966) by Helen Frankenthaler
AGE: 5–12 years
PROJECT DURATION: 90 minutes plus overnight drying

ABOUT THE ARTIST

Helen Frankenthaler (December 12, 1928–December 27, 2011) was an American painter from a prominent New York family. She is best known for developing her own innovative painting method known as soak-stain, a technique influenced by abstract painters such as Jackson Pollock. Soak-stain painting used diluted oil paint poured directly onto the canvas, creating vivid splashes of color. The paint would absorb into the raw canvas, becoming part of the material rather than drying on top of the surface. At the age of twenty-three, Frankenthaler's process of creating art led to a new school of painting known as Color Field Painting. She continued working with her soak-stain method throughout her more than sixty-year career.

SUPPLIES

- Heavyweight drawing paper
- Tempera paint (various colors)
- Paintbrush (medium round)
- Painting placemat

1. Start painting with warm colors such as yellow, peach, orange, magenta, and red first. Begin with the lightest warm color and work to the darkest. Paint irregular freeform shapes of color randomly around the paper, making sure to leave some white space in between for the cool colors. Do not create patches of the same or similar colors next to each other. Be sure to clean your brush on the placemat in between colors.

2. With a clean brush, repeat this process using cool colors. Cool colors are those such as green, blue, and purple. Start with the lightest cool color and work to the darkest. It's OK to leave a handful of white spaces if desired. Be sure to clean your brush on the placemat in between colors. Let dry overnight.

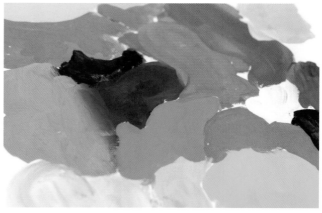

ADDITIONAL ARTWORK

Mountains and Sea (1952)

Canyon (1965)

Savage Breeze (1974)

FURTHER READING

Dancing Through Fields of Color: The Story of Helen Frankenthaler by Elizabeth Brown

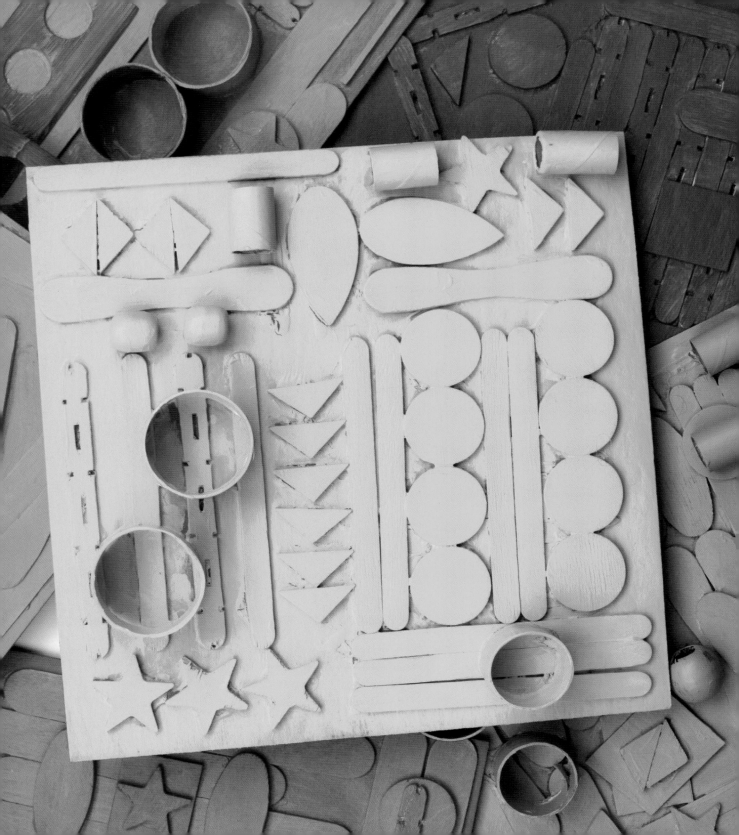

FOUND OBJECTS SCULPTURE

INSPIRED BY: *Big Black* (1963) by Louise Nevelson

AGE: 5-12 years

PROJECT DURATION: 90 minutes plus overnight drying

ABOUT THE ARTIST

American sculptor Louise Nevelson (September 23, 1899–April 17, 1988) was born in Russia, but moved to the United States at an early age. She is known for creating massive shadow box type installations constructed out of carefully arranged objects she found in city junk piles. Though she worked with a variety of materials, most of her sculptures are made of wood. The parts are stacked in a puzzle like an arrangement and are painted entirely in either black or white. Nevelson's artwork played an important role in the world of Feminist Art, challenging the idea that only men could create large-scale art.

SUPPLIES

- Cardboard or chipboard
- Tacky glue
- A variety of wooden pieces (Popsicle sticks, toothpicks, beads, craft shapes)
- A variety of cardboard recyclables (paper towel or toilet paper tubes cut into shorter pieces)
- Acrylic paint
- Paintbrush (large flat)
- Painting placemat

1. Gather together all of your wooden pieces and/or cardboard recyclables. Arrange them on the tabletop as you want them assembled on your final sculpture. Stack and layer your items to create a three-dimensional look.

2. Once you are happy with your design, use tacky glue to begin attaching the first layer of pieces to the cardboard. Continue until all the pieces have been glued in place. Let dry overnight before painting.

3. Choose one bright color of acrylic paint and paint over the entire sculpture. Cover the back-ground board and all parts completely with your paint to create a solid-color sculpture.

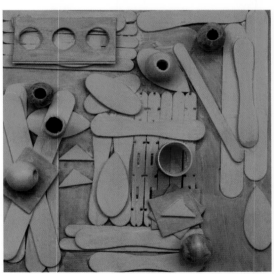
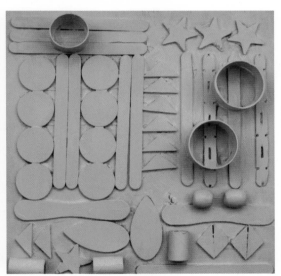

ADDITIONAL ARTWORK

Atmosphere and Environment X **(1969)**

Sky Jag IV **(1974)**

Sky Landscape **(1988)**

CIRCLES

INSPIRED BY: *Untitled 6F* (2008–2009) by Howardena Pindell
AGE: 5–9 years
PROJECT DURATION: 60 minutes plus overnight drying

ABOUT THE ARTIST

Howardena Pindell (April 14, 1943) is an African American abstract artist from Philadelphia, Pennsylvania. After studying art in college, she worked at the Museum of Modern Art, and taught at the State University of New York, Stony Brook. After Pindell moved to New York she began working with abstract shapes and collaging. She developed a unique style using layered dots. Different-sized hole punches are used to make dots from scrap paper, which she attaches to canvases in overlapping layers. She leaves the canvases unstretched and unframed, and nails them to the wall for display.

SUPPLIES

- Heavyweight drawing paper
- Various patterned papers (painted paper, wallpaper, scrapbook paper, or origami paper)
- Circle templates, tracers, and/or scrapbook-type large-hole punch
- Glue
- Scissors
- Pencil

1. Trace various sizes of circles on the back of the patterned papers. Tracing on the back will prevent having pencil marks on the patterned side once cut out. Circles can be traced using common items such as buttons, butter lids, bottle caps, and CDs. Using a variety of patterned papers will give your collage more interest.

2. Cut or punch out the circles. Large hole punches commonly found in the scrapbook section of craft stores are perfect for younger children to use.

3. Position the largest circles first on the drawing paper and work through to the smallest. The edges of the circles should overlap as you layer them, but not completely cover each other. Glue down the circles on the paper. Let dry overnight.

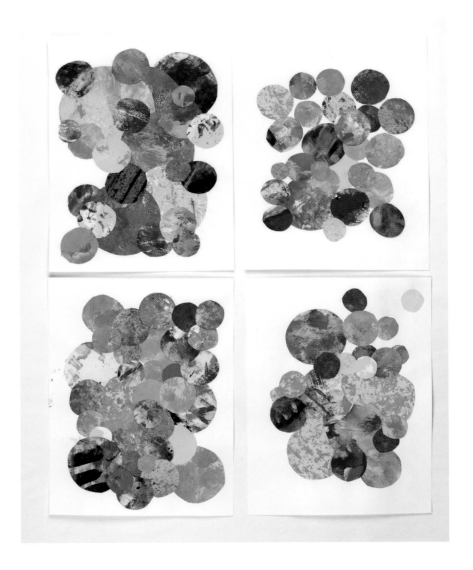

ADDITIONAL ARTWORK

Space Frame (1969)
Untitled #101 (1979)
Nautilus #1 (2014–2015)

ABSTRACT

INSPIRED BY: *Cossacks* (1910–1911) by Wassily Kandinsky
AGE: 5 years and up
PROJECT DURATION: 90 minutes plus overnight drying

ABOUT THE ARTIST

Born in Moscow, Russia, Wassily Kandinsky (December 4, 1866–December 13, 1944) originally studied law before becoming an artist. At age thirty he became a painter and began his career creating landscapes, but before long Kandinsky had the idea that paintings did not need to represent a specific subject or obvious scene. Instead art could be made using just shapes and colors alone. He felt that shapes could express feelings and colors could express music. With his new concept, he created the first abstract paintings using only color combinations, lines, and shapes. His pioneering ideas made him one of the founders of abstract art.

SUPPLIES

- Heavyweight drawing paper
- Tempera paint (black)
- Paintbrush (medium round)
- Chalk pastels
- Painting placemat

1. Make various lines, such as zigzag, diagonal, curved, and spiral, across the paper with black paint. Let dry overnight.

2. Use chalk pastels to add different patches of color next to the black lines. Begin with the lightest color chalk pastel first and work to the darkest. Add a rainbow somewhere on the paper. Make sure to leave plenty of white spaces; do not oversaturate your paper with color. When you are finished applying the chalk, use your fingertip to gently blend the chalk pastels.

TIP: To achieve clean and bright colors, blend each color using a different finger.

ADDITIONAL ARTWORK

Color Study: Squares with Concentric Circles (1913)

Moscow I (1916)

Composition X (1939)

FURTHER READING

Kandinsky (Basic Art Series 2.0) by Hajo Düchting

The Noisy Paint Box: The Colors and Sounds of Kandinsky's Abstract Art by Barb Rosenstock and Mary GrandPré

The Dreaming Giant: A Children's Book Inspired by Wassily Kandinsky by Veronique Massenot and Peggy Nille

COLORFUL CARDBOARD CREATIONS

INSPIRED BY: *Dan* (1973) by Alvin Loving
AGE: 5–12 years
PROJECT DURATION: 95 minutes plus overnight drying

ABOUT THE ARTIST

Alvin Loving (September 13, 1935–June 21, 2005) was an African American painter and collage artist from Detroit, Michigan. In 1968 he moved to New York City where he gained instant success thanks to his unique paintings of simple cube and hexagon shapes. After a few years of painting in this same style, Loving felt trapped and wanted a change. He turned his attention to creating collages—pieces of art made by sticking various materials together. As a young boy he would watch his mother and grandmother sew mismatched fabric scraps into beautiful quilts. These memories sparked his interest in making multilayered collages. His collages consist of torn pieces of painted cardboard, canvas, and paper. The pieces are arranged in overlapping shapes and patterns, forming large, free-flowing collages that reach out from the wall toward the viewer.

SUPPLIES

- Cardboard torn into pieces
- Tacky glue
- Tempera paint (various colors)
- Paintbrushes (medium round, large round)
- Painting placemat

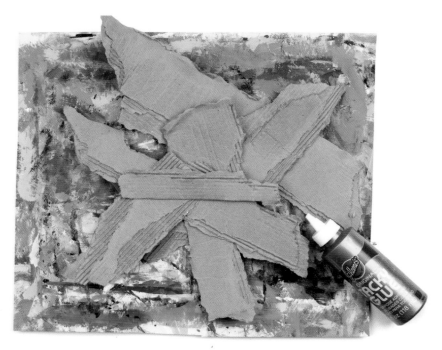

1. Tear pieces of cardboard into various shapes and glue them together with tacky glue. Make sure to overlap the cardboard pieces in different directions for an interesting collage.

2. Paint each piece of cardboard a different color. Let dry overnight.

TIP: Make sure to start with the lightest color first and wipe your brush on the placemat when moving onto a new color. This will prevent your colors from becoming muddy.

ADDITIONAL ARTWORK

Septehedron 34 (1970)

Wild Good Lake Series 3 (1980)

Beauty #58 (2005)

PRINTING WITH SPONGES

INSPIRED BY: *Composition II in Red, Blue and Yellow* (1929) by Piet Mondrian
AGE: 5–12 years
PROJECT DURATION: 90 minutes plus overnight drying

ABOUT THE ARTIST

Dutch painter Piet Mondrian (March 7, 1872–February 1, 1944) created a style of abstract art built solely on geometry and color. He wanted to create designs where the lines and colors were in perfect balance with each other. To do this, he drew only vertical and horizontal lines, and square and rectangle shapes. He restricted his color use to black, white, red, yellow, and blue. Mondrian's many grid-like paintings are easily identifiable and his influence extends into other areas of design in today's modern culture.

SUPPLIES

- Heavyweight drawing paper (9" x 12")
- Thin strips of construction paper (black)
- Precut sponges in various squares and rectangles
- Tempera paint (red, blue, yellow)
- Plate for paint
- Glue (sponges)
- Scissors
- Painting placemat

1. Cut different lengths of the black construction paper strips and glue them down on the drawing paper. The black strips should be positioned vertically and horizontally in a grid fashion. Tap the strips on a glue sponge for easy gluing.

2. Pour a small amount of each color paint on a plate. Keep the colors separated. Gently dip a precut sponge into the yellow paint. Wipe the excess paint on the edge of the plate so your sponge is not oversaturated. Begin stamping on the white paper. Continue this process using the red paint next and then the blue. Don't fill in all the shapes with paint. Leave a couple white spaces. Let dry overnight.

Option for Younger Artists

Glue precut construction paper squares and rectangles onto a white background paper. Dip the edge of a piece of cardboard into black paint. Stamp vertical and horizontal lines in between the squares and rectangles. Let dry overnight.

ADDITIONAL ARTWORK

Composition with Oval in Color Planes (1914)

New York City I (1942)

Broadway Boogie Woogie (1942–1943)

FURTHER READING

Mondrian (Basic Art Series 2.0) by Susanne Deicher

RAINBOW FIELDS

INSPIRED BY: *Wind, Sunshine, and Flowers* (1968) by Alma Woodsey Thomas
AGE: All ages
PROJECT DURATION: 60 minutes

ABOUT THE ARTIST

Alma Woodsey Thomas (September 20, 1891–February 24, 1978) was an African American painter and former middle school art teacher from Georgia. After retiring from teaching she enrolled in university art classes. There she learned about the Color Field movement, a style of art that focused on large expanses of color with very few details. Alma was in her seventies when she developed a unique style of painting, based on a mosaic pattern that used small, random brushstrokes in bright rainbow colors. Her use of color was her way of expressing beauty and happiness in the world. When she painted, Thomas liked to work in her kitchen or tiny living room, but failing health made it increasingly difficult for her to paint. She would place one end of the canvas frame in her lap and balance the rest against her leg or piece of furniture. This allowed her to rotate the canvas and paint the hard-to-reach areas. At the age of eighty-one, Thomas became the first African American woman to have her own art exhibit at the Whitney Museum in New York City.

SUPPLIES

- Heavyweight drawing paper (9" x 12")
- Tempera paint (a rainbow of colors)
- Paintbrush (medium round)
- Painting placemat

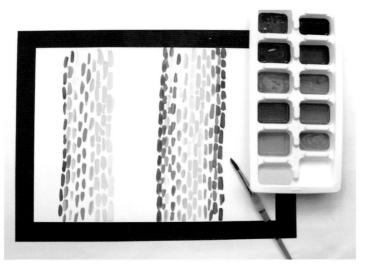

1. Warm Color Lines
   A. Begin with the color yellow. Create a grouping of three separate, parallel lines consisting of dashes. This first grouping should be on the left side of the paper. Make another grouping on the right side of the paper. Make sure to keep your lines straight. Clean your brush on the placemat when moving onto a new color.
   B. Repeat this process, making orange dashed lines on one side of each yellow grouping. Continue painting with pink, magenta, and red, making dashed lines next to the orange.

2. Cool Color Lines
   Once all the warm colors are done, start painting on the other side of the yellow groupings with green, blue, and purple to create a rainbow effect across the paper.

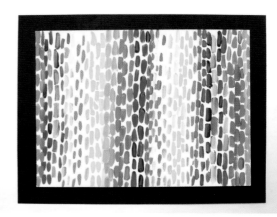

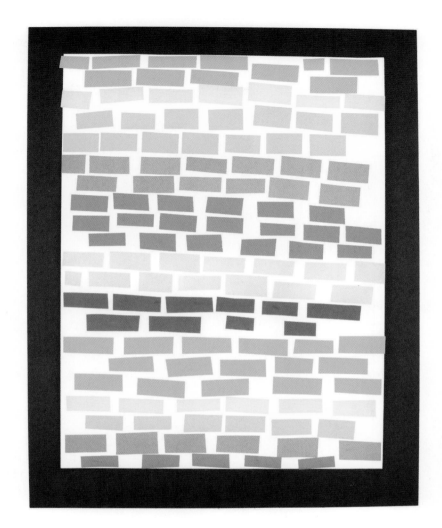

Option for Younger Artists

As an alternative to paint, use precut pieces of construction paper and glue them down into dashed rows of color.

ADDITIONAL ARTWORK

Red Abstraction (1960)

The Eclipse (1970)

Starry Night and the Astronauts (1972)

FURTHER READING

Alma Thomas by Ian Berry and Lauren Haynes

TISSUE PAPER DRIP DESIGNS

INSPIRED BY: *Volume Exhibition* by Maya Freelon

AGE: 5 years and up

PROJECT DURATION: 90 minutes plus overnight drying

ABOUT THE ARTIST

Maya Freelon (1982) is an African American artist who makes abstract sculptures from water-stained tissue paper. While living with her grandmother, Freelon discovered a pack of rainbow-colored tissue paper in her grandmother's basement. The paper had been damaged by dripping water, possibly from a leaky pipe, which caused the colors to bleed. Amazed and inspired by the staining, Freelon has used tissue paper in her creations ever since that first discovery. Her secret for producing the most interesting color flow is to let the water drip gently onto the paper so the color bleeds naturally, pushing the ink to the outer edges.

SUPPLIES

- Heavyweight drawing paper
- Tissue paper (bleeding)
- Liquid watercolors
- Paintbrush (medium round)
- Scissors
- Water
- Glue (sponges)

1. Prepare your tissue paper by dipping the paintbrush into liquid watercolors or plain water and drizzling it onto the folded tissue paper. Bleeding tissue paper works the best and will give a tie-dyed effect. Make sure not to oversaturate the paper. Let dry overnight.

2. Tear or cut the tissue paper into various sizes of squares. Crumple up the squares and gently tap them onto glue sponges. Press the tissue paper onto white heavyweight paper. Have fun exploring with the placement of the tissue paper.

ADDITIONAL ARTWORK

Synergy (2017)

Reciprocity Respite & Repass (2018)

ABSTRACT MARBLE PAINTING

INSPIRED BY: Jackson Pollock abstract paintings
AGE: 5-12 years
PROJECT DURATION: 45 minutes plus overnight drying

ABOUT THE ARTIST

Hailing from Cody, Wyoming, American painter Jackson Pollock (January 28, 1912–August 11, 1956) was the driving force behind the Abstract Expressionist movement of the 1950s. Abstract Expressionist artists work with only random splashes of color on canvas. To create his paintings, Pollock used a technique known as "drip" painting in which he let paint fall down onto canvases he laid out on the floor. Another method he used is called "action painting" in which paint is randomly thrown or poured onto the canvas. Large canvases were laid flat on the ground while Pollock moved quickly around them applying paint, sometimes flinging it with a stick directly from the can. Some of his paintings even have footprints on them from when he stepped in the wet paint.

SUPPLIES

- Construction paper (colored or white)
- Tempera paint (up to five colors)
- Shallow tray for holding paper
- Couple of marbles

1. Insert the construction paper into the tray. Drizzle dots of tempera paint on both the left and right edges of the tray overlapping onto the paper.

2. Drop marbles into the paint. Rock and tilt the tray back and forth so the marbles roll across the paper, creating lines and splatter marks. Continue until most of the paper is covered with paint. If additional paint is needed for the marbles, drizzle the same colors directly on the paper and continue the process.

3. Drizzle a new, contrasting color of paint directly on the paper. Rock and tilt the tray back and forth so the marbles spread the paint around the paper. Remove the finished painting and let dry overnight.

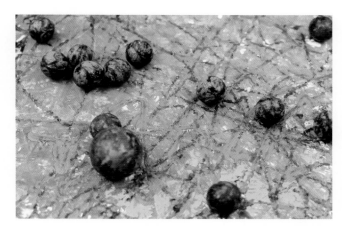

4. For a variety of abstract splatter paintings, repeat this process with a fresh piece of paper and different paint colors. This marble technique gives the look of the splatter paintings that Pollock is so famous for.

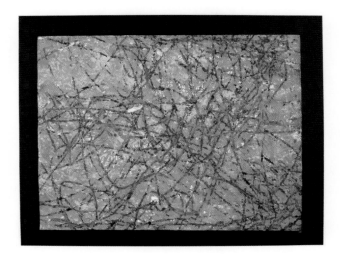

ADDITIONAL ARTWORK

Going West (1934-1935)

Mural (1943)

Autumn Rhythm: Number 30 (1950)

FURTHER READING

Jackson Pollock (Getting to Know the World's Greatest Artists) **by Mike Venezia**

Action Jackson **by Jan Greenberg and Sandra Jordan**

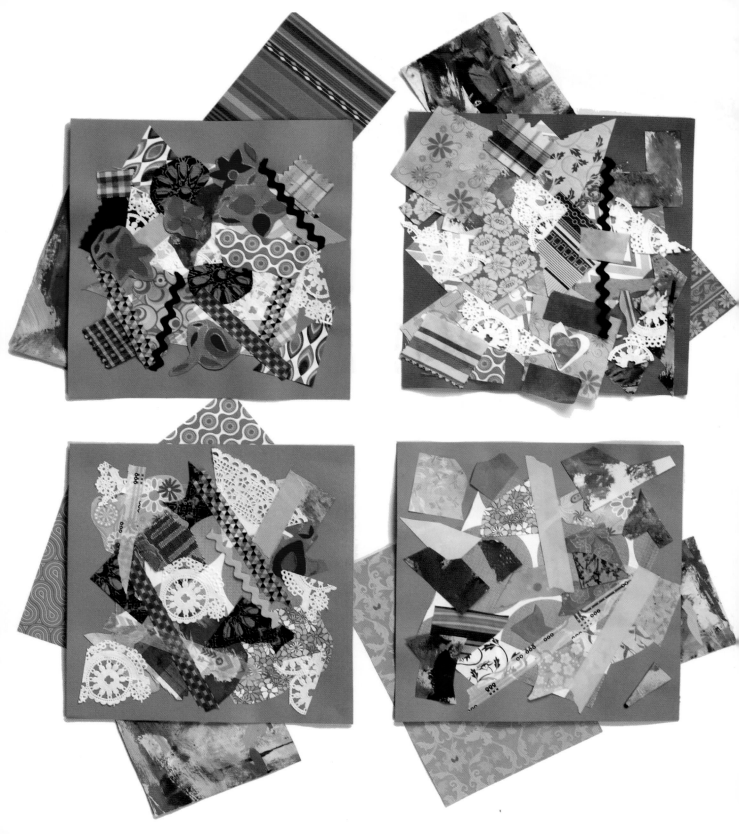

PATCHWORK COLLAGE

INSPIRED BY: *Explode* (1972) by Miriam Schapiro
AGE: 5 years and up
PROJECT DURATION: 90 minutes plus overnight drying

ABOUT THE ARTIST

Miriam Schapiro (November 15, 1923–June 20, 2015) was an artist from Toronto, Canada. She is known for her colorful collages, geometric patterned quilts, and abstract paintings. Her art often focuses on feminist issues and is a blend between traditional crafts and fine art. In the 1970s Schapiro developed a type of art known as femmage. Femmage art was strictly made by women and used collaged materials such as cloth, paint, fabric, and other textiles associated with women's household work. This led to her becoming a leader in the Pattern and Decoration movement, a short-lived style built on traditional craft methods like quilting, sewing, and appliqué. In the years since the Pattern and Decoration movement, Schapiro continued using fabric and craft techniques in her work as a way to bring attention to the role of women in American history.

SUPPLIES

- Large square construction paper (9" x 9")

- Origami paper (4" x 4")

- Scraps of painted paper and origami paper cut into irregular shapes

- Fabric scraps

- Glue (sponges)

- Scissors

- Paper doilies cut into irregular shapes, washi tape, fabric ribbons (optional)

1. Glue the origami paper onto the large square piece of construction paper. To create a collage of shapes, overlap the scraps of painted paper and origami paper, along with the paper doilies, onto the background paper. Glue down the pieces. Using glue sponges will prevent excess glue on your paper.

2. Use glue to affix fabric ribbons to the collage, then apply the washi tape to complete your masterpiece. Let dry overnight.

ADDITIONAL ARTWORK

Doll House (1972)

I'm Dancin' as Fast as I Can (1984)

Alexandra Exter (My Fan is Half a Circle) (1994)

FURTHER READING

Miriam Schapiro: Shaping the Fragments of Art and Life by Thalia Gouma-Peterson

CONCENTRIC CIRCLES

INSPIRED BY: *Abstract Composition with Semicircles* (1970) by Sonia Delaunay
AGE: 9–12 years
PROJECT DURATION: 120 minutes plus overnight drying

ABOUT THE ARTIST

Sonia Delaunay (November 14, 1885–December 5, 1979) was a Russian painter, illustrator, and fabric designer known for her abstract paintings composed of colorful geometric patterns. Her experiments working with colors and shapes started with a quilt she made for her baby son. She was inspired by the color and arrangement of the fabric pieces and began to apply the same concept to other objects. This led her into the areas of fabric and fashion design, interior decorating, and window displays. Delaunay's designs were groundbreaking and left a lasting impression on both international fashion and modern design.

SUPPLIES

- Heavyweight drawing paper
- Pencil
- Ruler
- Circle templates (various sizes)
- Oil pastels
- Baby oil
- Cotton swabs
- Painting placemat

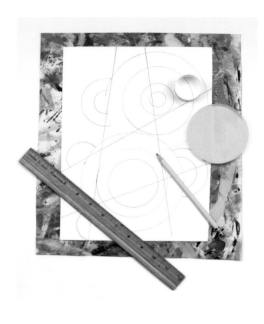

1. Making Concentric Circles
   A. Trace two large circles that slightly overlap each other. A small paper plate works great as a template. Within each of the large circles, trace a medium size circle. Within each medium circle, trace a smaller circle.
   B. Trace another medium-sized circle that overlaps the two large circles. Trace a smaller circle inside the medium circle.
   C. Trace two more smaller circles, one inside the other, anywhere on the paper. It's OK if any of the circles extend off the paper.
   D. Use a ruler and draw two to three random lines across the paper, dividing the circles into segments.

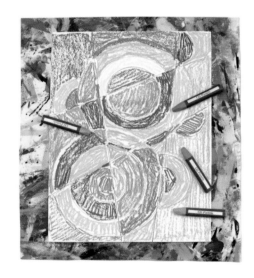

2. Completely color in each section with a different color of oil pastel. Do not use the same colors next to each other. Each time you come to a line, it creates a new section and should therefore be a different color. Consider using complementary colors, next to each other, like Delaunay is known for. Complementary colors are those opposite each other on the color wheel. (Refer to the color wheel on page 10.) The background areas outside the segments can be any color you choose.

3. Once all the various sections are colored in, use a cotton swab gently dipped once into baby oil to blend the oil pastels. Using baby oil will make the oil pastels look more like muted watercolors, and the use of heavyweight watercolor paper will keep the baby oil from soaking through. Start with the warm colors (yellow, orange, red) and blend the lightest color first, working in a circular motion. If the cotton swab runs dry, tap again once gently in the baby oil to remoisten the swab. After the warm colors have been blended, move to the cool colors (green, blue, purple), blending the lightest color first. It is not necessary to use a new swab when moving between light and dark colors, only when switching from the warm colors to cool colors. Let dry overnight.

ADDITIONAL ARTWORK

Fabric Pattern (Circles) (1928)
Composition 7 (1930)
Rythme (Rhythm) (1938)

FURTHER READING

Sonia Delaunay: A Life of Color by Cara Manes,
illustrated by Fatinha Ramos

159

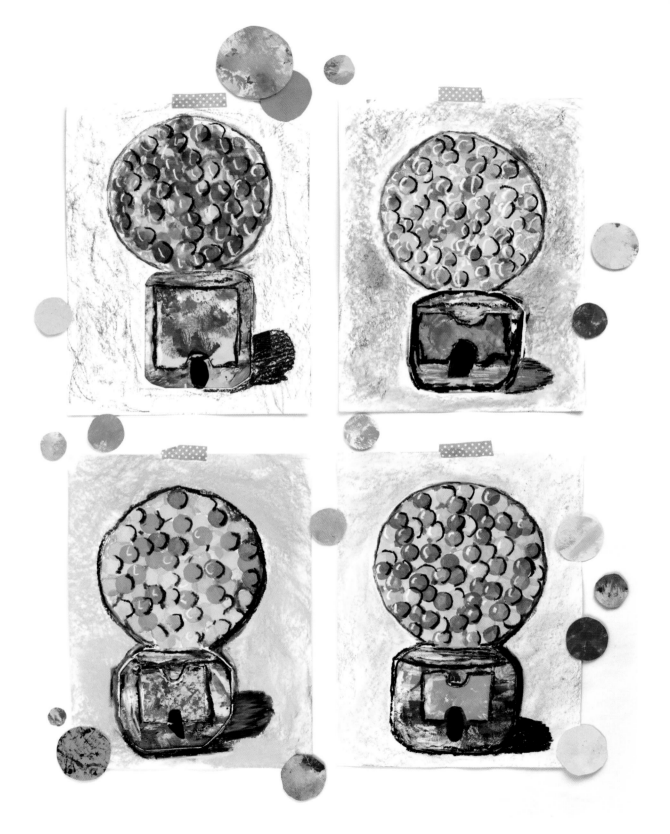

GUMBALL MACHINE

INSPIRED BY: *Three Machines* (1963) by Wayne Thiebaud
AGE: 7–12 years
PROJECT DURATION: 120 minutes

ABOUT THE ARTIST

Like many contemporary artists, American painter Wayne Thiebaud (November 15, 1920) started his career working in commercial art and graphic design. He is best known for his still-life paintings of food items such as cakes, pies, candies, and ice cream cones. His works are incredibly realistic looking, as if they were on display in a bakery window. This is due in part to his mastery at recreating detailed highlights and shadows. He also has a keen ability at transforming oil paint into the texture of the item it represents, for example, making it look like real icing. This is a feat made even more impressive considering that Thiebaud, unlike typical still-life artists, paints his subjects from memory or through sheer imagination.

SUPPLIES

- Heavyweight drawing paper
- Painted paper (small and medium squares)
- Scrap paper (black)
- Paint dot daubers, bingo markers, or large round markers
- Oil pastels
- Pencil
- Scissors
- Glue (sponges)
- Paper plate (small round)
- Painting placemat

1. Gumballs and Globe
   A. Trace around the paper plate on the white heavyweight drawing paper. Leave about three finger widths of white paper at the top. Use the paint daubers to create overlapping dots inside the circle. Make sure to keep the dots inside the pencil line. Fill the circle with a variety of colored dots.

2. Base
   A. Cut the corners of the medium piece of painted paper so they are rounded. Glue it down below the circle to create the base of the gumball machine.
   B. Cut a semicircle out of two opposing sides of the smaller piece of painted paper. It should represent an "H" after being cut. Glue on top of the center of the medium painted paper square with the curves positioned on the top and bottom.
   C. Cut an oval out of the black scrap paper. Glue it in the lower curve of the smaller piece to represent where the gumball comes out.

3. Highlights and Shadows
   A. Use oil pastels to create highlights and shadows on the gumballs and the base. The highlight is the lightest spot on an object. Use a white oil pastel to add the highlights on the upper left side of each gumball. Continue using the white oil pastel to make vertical lines down the left side of the base.
   B. The shadow is the darkest spot on the gumballs. Add the shadow on the right side of the gumballs. You don't have to put a shadow on each. Outline the right side of each gumball with a black oil pastel.
   C. Use the black oil pastel to outline the entire base. Make another horizontal line along the top edge of the "H," from one edge of the base to the other. Outline the "H" with black oil pastel. Make a few more vertical lines down the right side of the base. This will give the gumball machine base a three-dimensional look.
   D. Use a neutral color oil pastel, like tan or brown, to fill in any white space inside the globe where the dots did not cover.

4. Use a light color oil pastel such as beige, pink, or yellow. Peel off the wrapper and lay the oil pastel flat on the background paper. Drag it lightly around the white background. Use one finger to blend the oil pastel. Repeat this using another light oil pastel, but do not blend the color when finished.

5. Use a neutral color oil pastel such as gray or brown to outline the globe that holds the gumballs. Blend with one finger to create a softened edge. To create the shadow that is cast by the base, create an oval on the right side. Start about halfway up on the right side of the base and make a line that extends out, then curves down to the bottom of the base. Color in the oval and blend with one finger.

ADDITIONAL ARTWORK

Cakes (1963)

Two Paint Cans (1987)

Canyon Mountains (2011-2012)

FURTHER READING

Counting with Wayne Thiebaud by Susan Goldman Rubin

DINOSAUR JAZZ

INSPIRED BY: *Pez Dispenser* (1984) by Jean-Michel Basquiat
AGE: 9–12 years
PROJECT DURATION: 90 minutes plus overnight drying

ABOUT THE ARTIST

African American artist Jean-Michel Basquiat (December 22, 1960–August 12, 1988) was born to Haitian and Puerto Rican parents living in Brooklyn, New York. His rise to fame began in the late 1970s as part of a graffiti duo working in the Lower East Side of Manhattan. Basquiat's paintings brought graffiti artists to the attention of the New York City art gallery world. His art mixes elements of street art with more traditional approaches to painting. Much of his work is based on popular culture references, such as movies and cartoons, and expresses his views on social inequalities and injustices. Basquiat quickly became a celebrity in the art world, but his rise to fame and fortune only lasted for a short time due to his untimely death.

SUPPLIES

- Heavyweight drawing paper
- Painted paper or construction paper (two rectangular pieces in various colors)
- Glue (sponge or bottle)
- Scissors
- Oil pastels
- Pencil
- Tempera paint (dark colors)
- Paintbrush (medium round)
- Painting placemat

1. Using a pencil, draw a dinosaur that's the same shape as the one pictured in Basquiat's *Pez Dispenser* on heavyweight paper. Be sure to draw lightly. Create an oval head with an indent for the mouth. For the body, draw a wide banana or crescent shape that connects into the head. Add two arms to the body and two legs with triangular-shaped toes.

2. Fill in the body shape with black or other dark color paint. Let dry overnight.

3. Draw a crown on yellow painted paper or construction paper. Cut out the crown and glue it down above the dinosaur's head.

4. Make a line using white oil pastel to highlight the dinosaur's belly and back. Add details such as eyes, teeth, and nostrils to the dinosaur's head. Also add zigzag spikes down the dinosaur's back. Outline the various details, spikes, and crown with an additional contrasting color.

5. Use various oil pastels to make random patches of color around the dinosaur. On top of the oil pastels around the dinosaur, use black paint or black oil pastels to add fun designs, such as zigzags, spirals, and polka dots. These designs will add visual contrast to the background.

ADDITIONAL ARTWORK

Untitled (Skull) (1981)

Dog (1982)

Arm and Hammer II (1985)

FURTHER READING

Radiant Child: The Story of Young Artist Jean-Michel Basquiat by Javaka Steptoe

Life Doesn't Frighten Me by Maya Angelou, Jean-Michel Basquiat, and Sara Jane Boyers

CUBIST LOBSTER

INSPIRED BY: *Lobster and Cat* (1965) by Pablo Picasso
AGE: 9-12 years
PROJECT DURATION: 120 minutes plus overnight drying

ABOUT THE ARTIST

Pablo Picasso (October 25, 1881-April 8, 1973) was a Spanish painter, sculptor, printmaker, and one of the most influential artists of the twentieth century. He was such an experimental artist and created so many types of art that historians have categorized his art career into different stages. One of those stages, Cubism, is a style of art Picasso developed by blending influences he took from fellow artist Paul Cézanne and African sculpture. In Cubism, objects are painted from different angles all at once, so all sides are seen at the same time. The objects are usually represented as a jumble of fragmented geometric shapes. The lobster in this project is made using Cubist geometric shapes like those Picasso used.

SUPPLIES

- Heavyweight drawing paper
- Construction paper (various colors)
- Painted paper (brown, blue, green)
- Tempera paint (turquoise, dark blue, white)
- Paintbrush (medium round)
- Oil pastels (blues, white)
- Pencil
- Scissors
- Glue
- Painting placemat

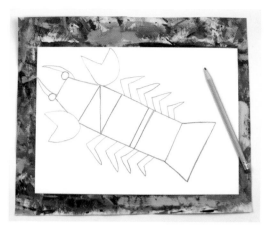

1. Drawing the Lobster
   A. In the center of the heavyweight paper, draw a rectangle on a diagonal. Leave room for the head, tail, and claws.
   B. Draw two trapezoids—one for the head and one for the tail.
   C. Divide the rectangle body into triangles and smaller rectangles.
   D. Add oval claws with a notched "V" in each.
   E. Add four legs to each side of the body. The legs should look like boomerangs and be about the thickness of a finger. If they are too thin, they will be hard to cut out.
   F. Add antennae protruding from each corner of the head. Make an eye at the base of each antennae, where the antennae and corner of the head meet.

2. Paint the lobster shapes with shades of blue and turquoise. Add white to the colors to create tints. Add patterns with the paint. Let dry overnight.

3. Cut out various rocks and seaweed plants from brown and green painted paper. Glue onto a piece of colored construction paper to be used as the background.

4. Cut out the lobster and glue it down on the background paper, overlapping the lobster on top of the rocks and seaweed. Create simple line designs using blue and white oil pastels on top of the painted lobster. Add a few more rocks and seaweed overlapping a bit on top of the lobster.

5. Use a little bit of white paint and fill in the background with some random brushstrokes. Keep the paint on the tip of your brush for a dry brush technique. Be careful not to get paint on your lobster.

ADDITIONAL ARTWORK

The Soup (1902-1903)
Bowl of Fruit, Violin and Bottle (1914)
The Three Musicians (1921)

FURTHER READING

Picasso and the Girl with a Ponytail by Laurence Anholt
Pablo Picasso: Breaking All the Rules by True Kelley
The Three Musicians: A Children's Book Inspired by Pablo Picasso by Veronique Massenot and Vanessa Hie
Pablo Picasso (Getting to Know the World's Greatest Artists) by Mike Venezia
Painting with Picasso (Mini Masters) by Julie Merberg and Suzanne Bober

CIRCUS ELEPHANTS

INSPIRED BY: *Elephants* (1976) by Alexander Calder
AGE: 7–12 years
PROJECT DURATION: 90 minutes

ABOUT THE ARTIST

Alexander Calder (July 22, 1898–November 11, 1976) was an American artist from Lawnton, Pennsylvania. He is best known for his wire figures and invention of the mobile, but he also created many paintings and massive outdoor sculptures. Calder loved the circus as a child. After moving to Paris in 1926, he created an entire mini-traveling circus made of wire and a variety of found materials. The circus was rigged so that he could manually operate it and give live performances. *Cirque Calder* gained him much acclaim. Throughout his life the circus would continue as themes in his art. Calder produced many sculptures, drawings, and paintings with acrobats, lions, and elephants as subjects. He often colored them using a simple color palette of red, yellow, blue, black, and white.

SUPPLIES

- Heavyweight drawing paper (9" x 12")
- Construction paper (red, blue, gray)
- Scrap paper (white)
- Tempera paint (black)
- Paintbrush (small round)
- Glue (sponges)
- Scissors
- Pencil
- Painting placemat

1. To make an elephant head, start by drawing a large heart with a rounded bottom roughly the size of a plum on a piece of construction paper. Cut out. To make the ears, cut a 3" x 5" strip from the same construction paper and fold the 5" length in half. Start at the fold and draw a letter "D." Open the paper and cut on the fold. This will give you two symmetrical ears. To make the trunk, draw a letter "J" the thickness of your finger on the same construction paper and cut out. Repeat this process using other colors of construction paper to create two additional elephants. To create the eyes, cut out two small circles from white scrap paper. Arrange all the parts on the large white background paper and glue them down.
   TIP: An easy way to create symmetrical eyes is to fold the white paper in half and draw one circle. Cut out the circle while the paper is folded to create two identical eyes.

2. Use black paint and a small round brush to add details such as wrinkles, eyebrows, and nostrils to the elephant faces. To emphasize the shapes of the faces, paint thin, black lines that follow the contour line of the shapes. Also add simple, fun designs on the white paper around the elephants. Zigzags, spirals, stars, and dots are some ideas for the background.

ADDITIONAL ARTWORK

Calder's Circus (1926–1931)

Fish (1944)

Blue, White and Red Target (1966)

FURTHER READING

Alexander Calder: Meet the Artist by Patricia Geis

Sandy's Circus: A Story About Alexander Calder
by Tanya Lee Stone and Boris Kulikov

Alexander Calder (Getting to Know the World's Greatest Artists)
by Mike Venezia

TALL, SKINNY PERSON

INSPIRED BY: *Man Pointing* (1947) by Alberto Giacometti
AGE: 9–12 years
PROJECT DURATION: 90 minutes plus overnight drying

ABOUT THE ARTIST

Alberto Giacometti (October 10, 1901–January 11, 1966) was a Swiss sculptor and painter known primarily for his sculptures of thin human figures. Giacometti moved to Paris in 1922 to pursue art but was forced to flee at the onset of World War II. Many people were left sad and poor after the war and this was reflected in the art of the time. This sadness can be seen in Giacometti's slender sculptures. He whittled his sculptures until they became elongated and withered figures, looking like freestanding, lonely skeletons. Many of his sculptures were cast in bronze, but Giacometti preferred working with plaster. Remnants of plaster and paint littered the studio where he lived, making it appear filthy and rundown. He carved the plaster so intensely that it would crumble to the floor. Only when he was happy with a sculpture would he paint it. By the 1960s Giacometti had gained worldwide attention with his unique version of the human form. He brought new life to traditional sculpture at a time when abstract art was the popular style.

SUPPLIES

- Craft sculpture wire (20 gauge) or thin wire clothing hangers
- Aluminum foil
- Modeling clay
- Acrylic craft paint (various colors)
- Paintbrush (large round)
- Painting placemat
- Scissors (optional)

1. Use two pieces of wire, both 24" long. To create a strong figure (armature), keep both pieces together. Fold both pieces in half so the ends are even. If they are not even, trim with scissors. Twist the folded ends a couple of times to make the head. Continue twisting one of the wires around the other, stopping where the arms will be located. This will make the form more stable. Leave the wire separated for legs. To make the arms, take a 12" piece of wire, folded in half, and twist around the main body where the legs separate. Take the four leg wires and twist two together to form a leg. Start wrapping small rectangles of foil around the wires to build up the body form.

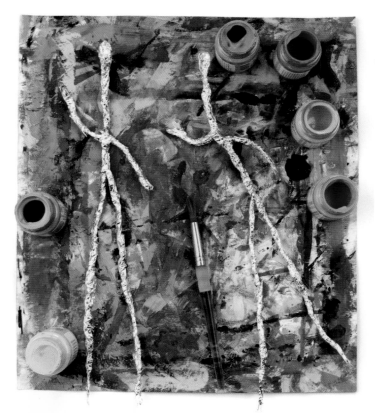

2. Use acrylic paint to paint on top of the foil. Let dry overnight.

3. Stand the dry, painted figure upright using colored modeling clay as a base.

ADDITIONAL ARTWORK

Gazing Head (1928)

The Artist's Mother (1950)

The Chariot (1950)

BARKING DOG

INSPIRED BY: *Red Dog* (1990) by Keith Haring
AGE: 8-12 years
PROJECT DURATION: 90 minutes

ABOUT THE ARTIST

Keith Haring (May 4, 1958-February 16, 1990) was an American graffiti artist, sculptor, and muralist from Pennsylvania. He began drawing as a boy, inspired by Disney cartoons and his father's illustrations. Haring moved to New York City to attend art school and quickly became involved as a graffiti artist. In the beginning he made white chalk drawings on black paper and posted them in the subways and public spaces. Using simple, cartoonlike images to spread his social and political messages made him a well-known figure. One of his most famous and often used icons is the dog, an image he began using in his early subway drawings. Haring's art gained mainstream commercial success in the 1980s and his images have become some of the most well recognized of the twentieth century.

SUPPLIES

- Cardboard or chipboard
- Small package of Model Magic or air dry clay
- Tacky glue
- Tempera paint (bright colors)
- Paintbrush (medium round)
- Scissors
- Painting placemat

1. Shape the clay into a ½″ thick flattened rectangle and position horizontally. Cut and remove a small triangle from the lower left corner of the clay. Cut this piece in half to make two small ears, and set aside. Make three additional evenly spaced vertical cuts along the bottom edge of the clay to define the legs. The area above the removed triangle will be the head. Make a small horizontal cut in the head to define the mouth. Gently spread apart the cut to open the mouth. Place the ears at the top of the head. In the upper corner opposite of the mouth, gently pinch and pull the clay to form the tail. **TIP:** Don't pinch or pull the clay too hard or it will distort your shape.

2. Position the dog in the center of the cardboard and glue it down using tacky glue.

3. Choose two colors of paint. Use one color for the dog, and one color for the background cardboard. Begin painting with the lightest of the colors first. Make sure to cover the cardboard completely so the paint is not streaky.

4. On the cardboard, use black paint to make a straight horizontal line under the dog. Add simple designs such as polka dots or dashes under the horizontal line. Outline the dog and add short diagonal lines near the mouth to represent the dog barking.

ADDITIONAL ARTWORK

Untitled (Dance) (1987)

Radiant Baby (1990)

Best Buddies (1990)

FURTHER READING

Keith Haring: The Boy Who Just Kept Drawing by Kay Haring and Robert Neubecker

Keith Haring Pop Art 123! by Mudpuppy

Keith Haring: I Wish I Didn't Have to Sleep by Desiree La Valette and David Stark

STILL LIFE WITH BIRD

INSPIRED BY: *Still Life with Parrot* (1951) by Frida Kahlo
AGE: 9–12 years
PROJECT DURATION: 90 minutes

ABOUT THE ARTIST

Frida Kahlo (July 6, 1907–July 13, 1954) was a painter from Coyoacán, Mexico, and is considered one of Mexico's greatest artists. Her paintings were influenced by Mexican art and culture and use a simple style of folk art images and brilliant colors. Kahlo was in a bus accident as a young woman and underwent many operations as a result. She was confined to her bed for months as she recovered. During this time, she began to paint. Art provided her a way to express her pain and deal with the limitations of her disabled body. She suffered from her injuries for the remainder of her life and at one point was in such pain that she was unable to leave her bed. To help raise money for her medical treatment, she produced several still-life paintings. Many of these vibrantly colored paintings depict the native Mexican fruits arranged on the table next to her bed. Kahlo also included the Mexican flag in several of her paintings as a way to honor her culture and heritage.

SUPPLIES

- Heavyweight drawing paper (9" x 12")
- Heavyweight drawing paper (small rectangle)
- Painted paper (medium rectangles in pink, orange, green)
- Painted paper (long, narrow rectangle in yellow)
- Painted paper scrap (brown)
- Scissors
- Pencil
- Glue (sponges)
- Chalk pastels
- Feather
- Painting placemat

1. Shapes
   Position the 9" x 12" heavyweight drawing paper horizontally. This will be the background paper. To create a watermelon, use a piece of pink painted paper. Draw a semicircle on the backside of the paper and cut out. Cut out small teardrop shapes out of brown painted paper and glue them onto the watermelon to represent the seeds. Draw a circle on the backside of orange painted paper to create an orange. Draw two long, large smiles on the back of light yellow painted paper to create two bananas. Draw an oval or football shape on the backside of darker yellow painted paper to create a lemon. Cut out all the shapes. Arrange them along the bottom of the background paper. Be sure to overlap some of the shapes. When you are happy with the arrangement, glue down the pieces. Draw a bird shape on a medium piece of white drawing paper. First draw a circle for the head and then a crescent shape for the body. Cut out the bird. Cut a fringe in the tail to represent feathers. Set the bird aside for step 3.

2. Background and Chalk Details
   A. Use chalk pastels to add details on the fruit. Create highlights and shadows where they would naturally be. To create a more realistic piece of fruit, draw a single line with the chalk on the edge of the fruit. Do not color the fruit in solid. Start with the lightest colors first and work toward the darker colors. Blend the lines on the fruit using a single finger. This smudge will make the fruit look more three-dimensional.

   B. Lightly draw a horizontal line across the paper to represent where the table and wall meet. Choose two colors of chalk—one color for the wall and a darker color for the table. Lay the chalks on their sides and lightly drag them across the paper. With one finger, gently blend the chalk around the area. Make sure not to get any chalk on the fruit shapes.

3. Bird
   Position the bird in front of the fruit and glue it down. Use a light tan chalk pastel and draw a line on the bird's belly to create a three-dimensional appearance. Blend the chalk with one finger. Make a black chalk pastel mark for the eye. Create a beak out of a scrap of orange painted paper. Glue a feather to the side and to the tail to complete the bird.

ADDITIONAL ARTWORK

Frieda and Diego Rivera (1939)
Self-Portrait with Bonito (1941)
Fruit of Life (1953)

FURTHER READING

Frida Kahlo and Her Animalitos by Monica Brown, illustrated by John Parra
Frida Kahlo: The Artist who Painted Herself by Margaret Frith, illustrated by Tomie dePaola
Who Was Frida Kahlo? by Sarah Fabiny
Frida by Jonah Winter and Ana Juan
Frida Kahlo (Little People, Big Dreams) by Maria Isabel Sanchez Vegara

BUMBLE BEES

INSPIRED BY: Maria Sibylla Merian's published insect illustrations
AGE: 9–12 years
PROJECT DURATION: 120 minutes

ABOUT THE ARTIST

Maria Sibylla Merian (April 2, 1647–January 13, 1717) was a nature artist and scientific illustrator from Germany. Her stepfather was an accomplished flower and still-life painter and taught her how to paint using watercolors. As a child she was fascinated with caterpillars and butterflies. She collected and studied different varieties of insects and plants, recording her observations in incredibly detailed illustrations. She discovered many new facts about plants and bugs and became an important figure in the scientific community. Merian published her first book of illustrations in 1670.

SUPPLIES

- Watercolor paper (7" x 12")
- Liquid watercolors (yellow and orange)
- Watercolor brush (medium round)
- Container of water to dilute the liquid watercolors, if needed
- Colored pencils (brown and yellow)
- Pencil
- Thin, permanent marker (black)
- Glitter glue or glitter paint
- Coarse table salt
- Painting placemat

1. The first bee will be painted from a symmetrical, bird's eye view, as seen from above.
   A. Position the watercolor paper vertically. Use a pencil to draw the bee's body. Draw an oval with a pointed end for the abdomen and add horizontal stripes. To create the thorax, add a fuzzy circle on top of the abdomen. Add a semicircle on the fuzzy thorax to represent the head. Add two smaller, attached semicircles for the eyes.
   B. Create symmetrical wings by drawing two long "M"s. Add one on each side with broken lines inside to represent the veins of the wings.
   C. Add jointed legs on each side of the fuzzy thorax. One pair should stretch upward from where the head meets the thorax. Two more pairs should stretch downward from where the thorax and the abdomen meet.
   D. Add antennae to the top of the head, branching off in between the eyes.

2. The second bee will be painted from a profile or side view.
   A. Create the bee's body by drawing an oval with a pointed end for the abdomen. Add stripes. To create the thorax, add a fuzzy circle on top of the abdomen. Add another pointed oval, with the point facing downward, attached to the fuzzy thorax to represent the head. Add one oval inside the head for the eye.
   B. Create one long heart shape for the wings. Position it sideways coming off the thorax. Put a line down the center of the heart and add broken lines to represent the veins of the wings.
   C. Add three jointed legs branching off the fuzzy thorax.
   D. Add an antenna to the top of the head.

3. Add Flowers
   A. To create a flower, start with an oval and add long finger like petals around the oval. Add a stem.
   B. Add thin lines from the oval downward on each petal to create a shadow effect.
   C. Use a thin, black permanent marker and trace over all the pencil lines. Short lines around the edge of the thorax will create a three-dimensional look. Use short black overlapping lines to fill in the stripes on the abdomen. Make sure to alternate by filling in every other stripe. Add overlapping dots with the permanent marker on one inside edge of the oval of the flower. Concentrate the dots in that area, gradually making fewer dots as you move away from the edge.

TIP: There are different shading techniques to create a three-dimensional look. One is using short overlapping lines known as cross-hatching. Another is to use overlapping dots and is called stippling.

4. Add Liquid Watercolor and Salt
Apply yellow liquid watercolor to the watercolor paper. Apply a little orange liquid watercolor to some of the yellow painted areas. Refrain from painting the wings. Next, sprinkle the watercolor paper with coarse table salt. The salt will absorb the watercolor and leave white marks on the paper, creating a unique bleeding effect. Once the watercolor paper dries, wipe off any excess salt.

5. Add Colored Pencil
Color the white areas of the thorax and abdomen with yellow colored pencil. Add brown colored pencil beginning around the edges of the thorax and getting lighter toward the center. Shade in the edges of the stripes with brown colored pencil.

6. Apply Glitter to the Wings
Paint the wings of the bees with glitter glue or glitter paint to create an iridescent effect.

ADDITIONAL ARTWORK

Metamorphosis of a Butterfly (1705)

Spiders, Ants and Hummingbird on a Branch of a Guava (1705)

Rote Lilie (1705)

FURTHER READING

To Maria Sibylla Merian: Artist, Scientist, Adventurer by Sarah B. Pomeroy and Jeyaraney Kathirithamby

The Girl Who Drew Butterflies: How Maria Merian's Art Changed Science by Joyce Sidman

BIRDCAGE

INSPIRED BY: *Merry Christmas Bird* (1956) by Andy Warhol
AGE: 7–12 years
PROJECT DURATION: 95 minutes plus overnight drying

ABOUT THE ARTIST

American artist Andy Warhol (August 26, 1928–February 22, 1987) was one of the most famous artists of modern times, reaching celebrity status not only for his artwork but also for his quirky personality. Originally from Pittsburgh, Pennsylvania, Warhol moved to New York City to become a commercial illustrator. He worked in a wide range of media including painting, drawing, sculpture, photography, and film, and he was a founder of the 1960s Pop Art movement, a style influenced by popular goods and entertainment. Warhol created a variety of art in his life but he is best known for his prints of advertising and media images, most notably Campbell's soup cans, Coca-Cola bottles, and brightly colored animals and celebrity portraits.

SUPPLIES

- Construction paper (9" x 12" in light colors)
- Small pieces of painted paper for bird body
- Scrap paper (white)
- Pencil
- Permanent marker (black)
- Scissors
- Tempera paint (black)
- Paintbrush (small round)
- Ruler
- Glue
- Chalk (neutral colors)
- Painting placemat

1. In pencil on the back of the painted paper, draw a bird's body by making either a triangular shape or a curving smile that comes to a point at the tail. Position the construction paper vertically and glue the cutout bird body in the center. Cut a triangle out of painted paper for the beak and glue it down. Cut a circle out of white paper for the eye and glue it down. Add a dot in the eye with a black permanent marker.

2. Use a ruler and pencil to draw a large box around the bird. Add straight vertical lines for the bars of the birdcage. The thickness of the ruler should be the spacing between the bars. Add a curved or triangular top and bottom to the birdcage. Fill in the top and bottom with simple designs such as spirals, curves, and scallops.

3. Paint over the pencil lines with black tempera paint. When painting the bars, make sure the lines go on top of the bird. Keep the paint light on your brush. Don't oversaturate it. Paint a small tail and legs on the bird. Use neutral color chalks to lightly shade the background area outside the birdcage. Blend with one finger to create a little bit of texture. Let dry overnight.

ADDITIONAL ARTWORK

25 Cats Name[d] Sam and One Blue Pussy (1954)

Flowers (1964)

Campbell's Soup I (1968)

FURTHER READING

Uncle Andy's Cats by James Warhola

Andy Warhol So Many Stars by Mudpuppy

Andy Warhol Happy Bug Day by Mudpuppy

Andy Warhol's Colors by Susan Goldman Rubin

Andy Warhol (Getting to Know the World's Greatest Artists) by Mike Venezia

Andy Warhol Andyland by Mudpuppy

PATTERNED PORTRAITS

INSPIRED BY: Kehinde Wiley portrait series
AGE: 7–12 years
PROJECT DURATION: 120 minutes plus overnight drying

ABOUT THE ARTIST

Kehinde Wiley (February 28, 1977) is a contemporary African American painter from Southern California. As a young boy growing up in Los Angeles, he attended local art classes, eventually studying at the Art Institute of San Francisco where he became skilled at painting. Wiley is gaining attention for his unique photo-realistic portraits of African American men and women. He blends the old with the new by dressing the models in modern, everyday clothes but posing them in an old-world style like that of traditional portraits. The backgrounds of his portraits are usually heavily patterned floral designs. Wiley even painted the official portrait of President Obama displayed at the Smithsonian's National Portrait Gallery.

SUPPLIES

- Construction paper (9" x 12" in various colors)
- Construction paper (6" x 9" in skin tones)
- Origami or printed scrapbook paper (4" x 8")
- Scrap paper (white)
- Strips and scraps of painted paper
- Tempera paint (various colors)
- Paintbrush (medium round)
- Washi tape or patterned paper
- Oil pastels (pink, tan, brown)
- Permanent marker (black)
- Pencil
- Scissors
- Glue (sponges)
- Painting placemat

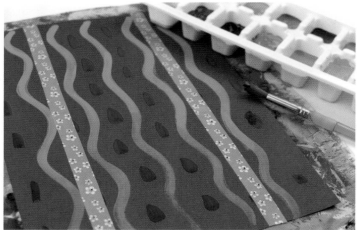

1. Position the 9" x 12" paper vertically. Paint one simple pattern across the paper. Make sure to leave space for a second alternating pattern, in a different color, in between the first pattern. Let dry overnight. Add a couple vertical strips of washi tape or patterned paper to the paper.

2. Creating the Head and Face
   A. Make the head out of a 6" x 9" piece of skin-tone colored construction paper. Draw a large oval for the head with two smaller ovals for the ears. Add a square or rectangle-shaped neck below the head. Cut out the head. Apply glue to the pencil-drawn side of the paper and position it in the middle of the patterned background paper.
   B. Add facial features. In the center of the face, horizontal with the ears, draw a "2" for the nose. Add a mouth. Use a small piece of white paper to create the eyes. Fold the paper in half and draw an oval. Keep the paper folded while cutting out to create two symmetrical eyes. In the same way, create two circles for the irises out of colored construction paper or painted paper. Fold the paper, draw a circle, and cut out while the paper is folded. Add a pupil to each circle with black permanent marker. Glue down the eye pieces onto the face. Using a glue sponge will keep glue spills and marks to a minimum.

C. Add the hair. Cut construction paper or painted paper into strips. Position them around the top of the head, overlapping them for a more realistic look. Glue down the strips.

D. Add a shirt. With a 4" x 8" piece of patterned paper positioned horizontally, cut a V-neck or crew (curved) collar in the center of the longer 8" side. Cut a slight curve on each top corner of the paper to create shoulders. Glue it down at the base of the neck. Trim any excess paper from the bottom of the shirt that overhangs the background paper.

E. With oil pastels, shade lightly around the nose, ears, and chin to create a shadow. Tan, pink, or light brown oil pastels work the best. Choose an oil pastel that is darker than your chosen skin tone paper. Create a shadow where the chin and neck meet by drawing a short horizontal line on each side of the neck just below the chin. Take one finger and blend the oil pastels down toward the shirt.

3. Add Leaves
Cut leaf shapes out of painted paper or colored construction paper. Glue them down on the background around the portrait.

ADDITIONAL ARTWORK

Napoleon Leading the Army Over the Alps (2005)

Randerson Romualdo Cordeiro (2008)

Portrait of Barack Obama (2017)

OPEN WINDOW TO THE SEA

INSPIRED BY: *Open Window, Collioure* (1905) by Henri Matisse
AGE: 9–12 years
PROJECT DURATION: 90 minutes

ABOUT THE ARTIST

Henri Matisse (December 4, 1866–December 13, 1944) was a French painter, sculptor, and collagist who was a leading member of the Fauves, a group of artists known for using vibrant, unnatural colors and exaggerated forms. The colors the group used were so "unnatural" that many people disliked their style of painting. He and similar artists were nicknamed Fauves, meaning "wild beasts" in French. Matisse's *Open Window, Collioure* is an early example of a Fauve style painting with its thickly applied, unmixed colors. He spent many summers in the small fishing town of Collioure, France, located on the Mediterranean Sea where he created several paintings of the view from his room looking out to the water. Fauvism declined in the early 1900s but Matisse's work still gained interest. He worked in many different art styles throughout his career, such as cut paper, mosaics, sculpture, and printmaking. His influential use of vibrant colors and his legacy as a prominent artist of the twentieth century continues on today.

SUPPLIES

- Construction paper (9" x 12" in light colors)
- Heavyweight drawing paper (4" x 6")
- Ruler
- Pencil
- Glue
- Tempera paint (various colors)
- Paintbrush (medium round)
- Painting placemat

1. Creating the Window and Shutters
   A. Place a piece of 9" x 12" construction paper in a vertical position. To create the window, position the 4" x 6" white paper vertically and glue it down on construction paper, approximately 2" below the top edge.
   B. Create shutters by drawing two narrow trapezoids, one on each side of the window. Align the ruler along the left side of the white paper. Down the right side of the ruler, draw a line approximately 7.5" long. This line should start at the top edge of the white paper and end about 1.5" below the white paper. Down the left side of the ruler, draw a line approximately 9.5" long. This line should start about 1" above the white paper and end about 2.5" below the white paper. Draw a line connecting the tops of the two lines and another connecting the bottoms of the two lines. Reverse this process and repeat it on the right side of the white paper to make the second shutter. Once both shutters are drawn, add trapezoid and parallelogram shapes inside each.

2. Begin painting the window view on the white paper. To make the sailboats, make a vertical line with a small curve underneath. Add more horizontal lines for grass, sand, and water, and short brushstrokes at the top for the clouds.

3. Paint flower pots and plant containers below the open window between the shutters. Paint the shutters and the geometric shapes inside. Fill in the area around the window shutters with patches of various colors, making sure not to over blend.

ADDITIONAL ARTWORK

Goldfish (1911)

Basket with Orange (1913)

Codomas (1943)

FURTHER READING

The Iridescence of Birds: A Book About Henri Matisse by Patricia MacLachlan and Hadley Hooper

Matisse's Garden by Samantha Friedman and Henri Matisse

Henri Matisse: Drawing with Scissors (Smart About Art) by Jane O'Connor and Jessie Hartland

A Bird or Two: A Story About Henri Matisse by Bijou Le Tord

Blue and Other Colors: with Henri Matisse (First Concepts With Fine Artists) by Henri Matisse

The Mermaid and the Parakeet: A Children's Book Inspired by Henri Matisse by Veronique Massenot and Vanessa Hie

CITY BUILDINGS

INSPIRED BY: *Castle and Sun* (1928) by Paul Klee

AGE: 5–9 years

PROJECT DURATION: 90 minutes plus overnight drying

ABOUT THE ARTIST

German painter Paul Klee (December 18, 1879–June 29, 1940) was born in Switzerland to a Swiss mother and German father. As a boy his family encouraged his imagination and his love for art and music. In 1911 he joined Der Blaue Reiter (The Blue Rider), a group of artists interested in sharing their spiritual truths through art. Though he is considered one of the founders of modern art, his work cannot be classified into any one style of art. Klee became a highly influential artist and taught for a while at the revolutionary Bauhaus art school. Not long after, Germany began labeling all modern art as degenerate and banned it from their museums. The Bauhaus school was eventually closed by the police, Klee's studio was searched, and he left Germany to live in Switzerland. His style has a simplistic, childlike quality of simple lines, bold colors, and geometric shapes.

SUPPLIES

- Heavyweight drawing paper
- Painted paper or construction paper (squares and rectangles in various colors)
- Chalk pastels
- Glue (sponges)
- Scissors
- Small rectangle of cardboard for scraper/stamper
- Tempera paint (black)
- Painting placemat

1. Position the drawing paper horizontally. Lay out the painted paper shapes to make stacked buildings. Use rectangles and squares for the base of the buildings and cut triangles from leftover square shapes for the roofs. Cut out a circle from a square piece of paper for the sun. Glue down the shapes when you are pleased with your design layout.

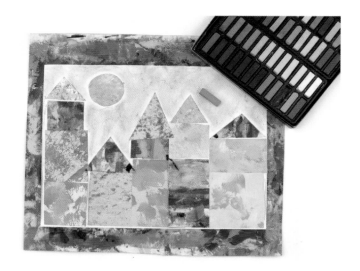

2. On the background paper around the buildings, use one color of chalk pastel and gently shade in the sky. Use one finger to blend the chalk around the sky.

3. To add the line details, take the cardboard scraper/stamper and gently tap the short edge into black paint. Take the end of the dipped cardboard and stamp lines on the edges of all the shapes. Let dry overnight.

ADDITIONAL ARTWORK

Senecio (1922)

Growth of Night Plants (1926)

Cat and Bird (1928)

FURTHER READING

The Cat and Bird by Geraldine Elschner and Peggy Nille

Paul Klee: Painting Music by Hajo Düchting

Paul Klee: Life and Work by Boris Friedewald

Dreaming Pictures: Paul Klee (Adventures in Art) by Jürgen von Schemm

Paul Klee (The Life and Work of) by Sean Connolly

Paul Klee (Getting to Know the World's Greatest Artists) by Mike Venezia

TRAMP STEAMER

INSPIRED BY: *Tramp Steamer* (1908) by Edward Hopper
AGE: 9-12 years
PROJECT DURATION: 95 minutes plus overnight drying

ABOUT THE ARTIST

Edward Hopper (July 22, 1882-May 15, 1967), who hailed from Nyack, New York, is one of America's most popular and influential painters. Encouraged by his parents to pursue art, he studied illustrating in art school before switching to painting. Hopper was a great observer of his surroundings. As a Realist painter he had the unique ability to paint everyday life in a natural, realistic looking way. He was also skilled at painting light in a way that gave his work an atmosphere of loneliness, whether it be a city scene, country landscape, or waterside view. Hopper created more than eight hundred oil and watercolor paintings during his career and was also chosen to represent the United States in an international exhibition in Italy. In 1961 his artwork was selected by Mrs. Kennedy for display in the White House.

SUPPLIES

- Heavyweight drawing paper (12" x 18")
- Construction paper (3" x 12" in black)
- Construction paper (1" x 12" in red)
- Painted paper (1.5" x 4" in yellow/brown)
- Scrap paper (1.5" x 2.5" in white)
- Tempera paint (blue, green, turquoise, yellow, orange, white)
- Paintbrushes (medium flat, large flat)
- Oil pastels (neutral colors)
- Glue
- Pencil
- Scissors
- Small rectangle of cardboard for scraper/stamper
- Paint container
- Painting placemat

1. Background
   A. Start with two analogous colors of oil pastels like yellow/gold or yellow/orange. Analogous colors are colors next to each other on the color wheel. (Refer to the color wheel on page 10.) Unwrap the oil pastels and lay them flat on the 12" x 18" white heavyweight drawing paper. Drag the oil pastels across the top half of the paper.
   B. Use a large flat brush to paint the water on the bottom half of the paper with both light and dark shades of blue paint. Use large brushstrokes to give movement to the water. Let dry overnight.

2. Boat
   A. To make the boat hull, take the 3" x 12" black construction paper and draw two 3" rectangles with rounded bottom corners, along the top edge of the paper. Cut out the rectangles. Keep the scraps. Glue the 1" x 12" strip of red construction paper along the bottom of the hull.
   B. To make the smokestack, glue the 1.5" x 4" piece of yellow/brown painted paper to the backside of the center of the boat with the painted paper side exposed. Take one of the black rectangle scraps and cut it down to the width of the smokestack. Glue it onto the top of the smokestack.

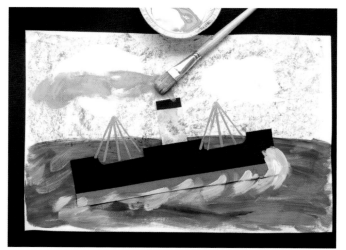

3. Details
   A. Glue the ship onto the background paper, making sure the ship is angled in the water.
   B. Use white paint and a medium flat brush to paint white clouds in the sky. Use a large flat brush and blue paint to add waves. Use overlapping brushstrokes to make waves splashing up on the side of the boat. Dip the tip of the brush into white paint and create a tint to represent whitecaps in the water. Clean your brush on the placemat.
   C. Paint the ship support lines by dipping the long edge of a cardboard scraper/stamper

into a mix of yellow and orange paint. Carefully place the edge of the cardboard on the paper and make three to five lines that extend from a central point down to the boat. There should be one group of lines at each cutout on the top of the boat.

D. Use leftover paint from the support wires and paint large plumes of smoke trailing from the smokestack.

4. Cut two small oval windows from the 1.5" x 2.5" piece of white scrap paper. Glue them just below the smokestack on the side of the boat.

ADDITIONAL ARTWORK

House by the Railroad (1925)
Gas (1940)
Nighthawks (1942)

FURTHER READING

Edward Hopper (Getting to Know the World's Greatest Artists) by Mike Venezia and Sarah Mollman Underhill
Edward Hopper Paints His World by Robert Burleigh and Wendell Minor
Edward Hopper: Summer at the Seashore (Adventures in Art) by Deborah Lyons and Edward Hopper

CITY LIFE IN HARLEM

INSPIRED BY: *Harlem* (1946) by Jacob Lawrence
AGE: 9–12 years
PROJECT DURATION: 90 minutes plus overnight drying

ABOUT THE ARTIST

African American painter Jacob Lawrence (September 7, 1917–June 9, 2000) was a young boy when he moved to the Harlem area of New York. Inspired by his life there, he created his art as a way to share the African American experience with others, telling stories of their history and struggles. He often spanned his colorful paintings over multiple individual panels. When the panels were arranged together, they formed a complete story. At the age of twenty-three he became popular when he displayed a massive sixty-panel work titled *Migration Series*. Lawrence was one of the first African American artists to gain such mainstream attention.

SUPPLIES

- Heavyweight drawing paper
- Construction paper rectangles (white, red, black, brown, burgundy)
- Construction paper strips (white, black)
- Tempera paint (various colors)
- Paintbrush (large flat)
- Glue (bottle or sponges)
- Scissors
- Permanent marker (black)
- Oil pastels (white, black, brown)

1. Creating the Background and Buildings
   A. Position the heavyweight paper horizontally. Paint the sky a lighter color. The sky should cover approximately the top three-quarters of the paper.
   B. Paint the ground area brown. The ground should cover the bottom quarter of the paper. Let dry overnight.
   C. Glue down colored construction paper (red, black, brown, and burgundy) rectangles so that they touch the brown ground. Make sure to layer your buildings so they overlap each other for a staggered look. Cut out notches along the top of the white rectangle, then glue it down in the center of the paper.

2. Adding the Details
   A. Cut the white and black construction paper strips into narrow rectangles for the windows. Glue down the windows in rows on your buildings to represent the different floors.

   TIP: Using pre-moistened glue sponges helps keep excessive glue off the projects. Just tap your precut shapes onto the cut sponges soaked with glue. This is perfect for collage projects and younger students.
   B. Use a black marker to add details such as staggered bricks, window details, and fire escape ladders to the buildings.

   C. Use white, black, and brown oil pastels to add highlights such as outlining the windows and building edges.
   D. Any leftover scrap paper can be used to add cars, clouds, and a sun to your city scene.

Option for Younger Artists

Paint rectangular pieces of cardboard with red, brown, or black tempera paint. Use oil pastels to add details such as windows and doors. Stand the buildings upright using modeling clay as a base.

ADDITIONAL ARTWORK

This is Harlem (1943)

A Family (1943)

The Builders (1980)

FURTHER READING

Jacob Lawrence (Getting to Know the World's Greatest Artists) by Mike Venezia

Jacob Lawrence in the City by Susan Goldman Rubin

Jake Makes a World: Jacob Lawrence, A Young Artist in Harlem by Sharifa Rhodes-Pitts and Christopher Myers

Story Painter: The Life of Jacob Lawrence by John Duggleby

FERRIS WHEEL IN PARIS

INSPIRED BY: *The Big Wheel* (1911–1912) by Marc Chagall
AGE: 9–12 years
PROJECT DURATION: 120 minutes plus overnight drying

ABOUT THE ARTIST

Russian-born artist Marc Chagall (July 7, 1887–March 28, 1985) was the oldest of nine children from a Jewish family. Over the course of his life he spent time living in Belarus, France, and the United States. He worked in several formats including painting, illustrating, murals, ceramics, and stained glass. His brightly colored paintings have a dream-like quality to them, sometimes referred to as supernatural. Chagall drew inspiration from a variety of sources including Russian folktales, his Jewish heritage, the theatre, and the circus. In 1910 he left Russia and moved to Paris, considered to be the center of modern art. *The Big Wheel* is his first painting inspired by his Paris surroundings.

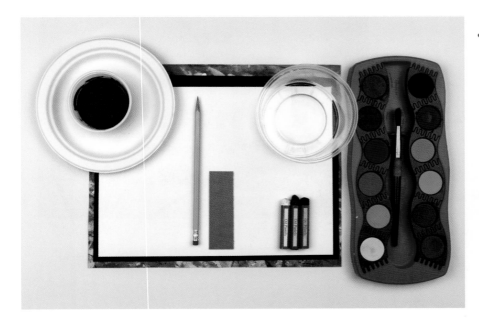

SUPPLIES

- Watercolor paper (9" x 12")
- Paintbrush (medium round)
- Tempera paint cake or tempera paint (various colors)
- Container of water
- Pencil
- Small plate for circle tracer
- Oil pastels
- Small rectangle of cardboard for scraper/stamper
- Tempera paint (black)
- Painting placemat

1. Background Paper
   Position a piece of watercolor paper horizontally. With a paintbrush, apply a warm color paint, such as yellow, on one side of the paper. Then add a small rectangle at the bottom of the paper on the opposite side, using the same warm color. Apply a cool color paint, such as blue, on the other side of the paper. Add a couple of clouds to each area. For example, create cool color clouds on the warm color side and warm color clouds on the cool color side. Add dark blue paint at the bottom of the paper, making sure not to paint over the small yellow spot. This will become the city. Let dry overnight.

2. Eiffel Tower, Ferris Wheel, and City of Paris
   A. To create the Eiffel Tower, lightly sketch an elongated triangle in pencil on the left-hand side of the paper. Add a lowercase "m" at the bottom and fill in the tower structure with sections of vertical and horizontal lines.
   B. To create the Ferris wheel, lightly trace around a small plate on the upper right side of the paper. The bottom of the circle should just touch the dark blue area where the city will be drawn.
   C. Add rectangles and squares to the right-hand side of the dark blue area for the buildings. Add the word "Paris" to the yellow rectangle at the bottom of the left-hand side of the paper.

   D. Use black or brown oil pastels to trace over all of the pencil lines. Add details to the Ferris wheel such as the support beams and passenger cars (Ferris wheel bucket seats). Add short vertical lines in the Eiffel Tower. Adding white to certain areas will give the shapes highlights. White oil pastels can also be used to create clouds and building windows.

3. Ferris Wheel Spokes

    Gently tap the longer edge of a cardboard scraper/stamper into the black tempera paint. Stamp lines in a radial pattern around the large circle. **TIP:** Pour a thin line of black paint on a paper plate to make stamping easier. Let dry overnight.

ADDITIONAL ARTWORK

I and the Village (1911)

Paris Through the Window (1913)

The Green Violinist (1923–1924)

FURTHER READING

Through the Window: Views of Marc Chagall's Life and Art by Barb Rosenstock and Mary GrandPré

A Picture for Marc by Eric A. Kimmel and Matthew Trueman

Papa Chagall, Tell Us a Story by Laurence Anholt

Journey on a Cloud: A Children's Book Inspired by Marc Chagall by Veronique Massenot and Elise Mansot

MATERIALS FOR MASTERPIECES

Art supplies are important. Use the best high-quality art materials you can afford. Having the right supplies and understanding how to use those supplies and materials helps create creative confidence in children.

PAPER

TIP: For younger children, consider using smaller pieces of paper. This will keep children from getting overwhelmed by the size of the paper.

- Heavyweight drawing paper—80-90 lb. paper works best. It holds the paint well and does not wrinkle.

- Heavyweight construction paper—I prefer a heavyweight construction paper because it holds the weight of tempera paint when creating painted paper. The paper should contain strong fiber that is tough enough for folding and curling without tearing, and should be fade-resistant in bright colors. My favorite brand is Tru-Ray construction paper.

- Watercolor paper—liquid watercolor paint has a great effect on a good-quality watercolor paper.

- Tissue paper—bleeding and non-bleeding.

PAINT

- A good tempera paint is necessary for a great piece of artwork.

- I am often asked which tempera paint is my favorite. I always choose premium tempera paint. The pigment is much stronger than other paints. I also like to use tempera cakes.

- Liquid watercolors are awesome. I store them in plastic food containers with snap-on lids. Two watercolor techniques that I like to use are wet on wet, and applying coarse table salt.

- Watercolor pan sets.

- Paint daubers (stampers). These make great colored dots.

- Ink daubers (such as Bingo Bottle Refillable Markers) are good for outlining or filling in shapes.

- Tempera paint sticks.

- Inexpensive acrylic paint found where craft supplies are sold.

PAINTBRUSHES

- Large flat brushes are great for transferring paint to a large piece of construction paper. They also work well for younger children to use.

- Small and medium flat brushes work well for smaller projects, yet still give a great texture when painting landscapes.

- Small and medium round brushes are perfect for outlining shapes and applying designs. They also work great with liquid watercolors and tempera cakes.

- Large round brushes are ideal for creating painted paper.

OTHER OPTIONAL PAINTING TOOLS

- Foam texture brushes give a wonderful overall texture.

- Cardboard scrapers are an awesome tool for creating the look of painted wood. Scrapers make bold lines when dragged across paper.

- Spray bottles filled with watered down paint are wonderful at making magical snow, knots in a piece of wood, or stars in space.

- Inexpensive cleaning tools for the home such as kitchen sponges, scouring pads, dusters, bathroom brushes, and body scrubbers make great texture tools when dipped in a tray of tempera paint.

- Brayer rollers are used to rub out paint on paper, or for printmaking.

- Packing material/foam pipe insulation cut at one end, rolled and secured with a rubber band, is another great texture tool.

- Texture brushes and foam paint rollers can also be purchased from educational supply stores.

- Oversized paintbrushes from home improvement stores.

DRAWING

- Markers
- Colored pencils
- Oil pastels
- Metallic oil pastels
- Chalk pastels
- Permanent markers (chisel, fine, extra-fine tips)
- Watercolor crayons

SCRAP BOX COLLAGE MATERIALS

- Pom-poms
- Sequins
- Glitter
- Small paper plates
- Chipboard, cardboard sheets, and tubes
- Wire
- Tin foil
- Washi tape
- Colored masking tape
- Fabrics
- Ribbons
- Wooden pieces (Popsicle sticks, toothpicks, beads, craft shapes)
- Old calendars, catalogs, greeting cards, and magazines are also great for inspiration and collage materials

ARTIST TOOLS

- Glue
- Tacky glue
- Pencil
- Ruler

- Scissors
- Glue sponges—Children can get easily discouraged by using liquid glue. An easy solution is to cut a kitchen sponge in half and place in a shallow plastic lunch container so that the sponge sits flush with the top edge of the container. Pour glue on top of the sponge and seal the container with the lid so the sponge stays moist and does not dry out. Children can tap their paper onto the sponge to transfer the glue without having glue puddles on their artwork. Spray sponges every couple months with mouthwash to prevent mold.

CLAY TOOLS

- Air dry clay
- Modeling clay
- Jazz Gloss tempera paint
- Wooden tools (skewer, Popsicle stick, small rolling pin)
- Metal kitchen scraper for cutting clay
- Small water container

INDEX

ABOUT THE AUTHOR

LAURA LOHMANN has a master's degree in art education, a minor in art history, and has been an elementary school art teacher for 25 years. She lives in Ohio with her husband, two adventurous children, and one adorable golden doodle pup. She started her blog Painted Paper Art in 2010 to share her love of creating art with children. Laura and her family love spending time in nature, and they especially enjoy exploring America's national parks. She is always painting with her students and loves creating new and colorful projects. Her work has been featured in *Arts and Activities* and *Family Fun Magazine* among others. *Mini Masterpieces: Exploring Art History With Hands On Projects For Kids* is her first book.

PAINTEDPAPERART.COM   f **PAINTEDPAPERART**   ◎ **PAINTEDPAPERART**